KISSES OF
CALVARY
& OTHER SERMONS

JACK HYLES

This book is given as part of
a gift package by:

PS  2011

Name Felicia Smith

Address 1265 BlueBell Trail

City Schererville State IN Zip 46375

Dedicated to my mother,
MRS. C. M. HYLES,
a great preacher—one who has never preached
behind a pulpit, but whose life has been one great sermon.

ISBN: 978-0-9819603-9-5

First Printing — 2011

10 sermons preached in 1965 by Dr. Jack Hyles

To order additional books by Dr. Jack Hyles,
please contact:
Prepare Now Resources
507 State Street
Hammond, Indiana 46320
219-932-0711

hylespublications.com
info@hylespublications.com

Contents

The worse thing that can happen to any of us is to have a path that's made too smooth. One of the greatest blessings the Lord ever gave us was a Cross.

– Charles Haddon Spurgeon

Introduction

Introduction

It is one of the greatest joys of my life to write the introduction of this book written by my son. You will find in him a person who always has time and love for his mother, wife, children, church family, and young preachers.

This is the Jack Hyles I have watched grow from boyhood to manhood, giving Christ first place in his life and always having a great love and burden for lost souls.

My son and his work have always been very dear to me through the years. My prayer is the Lord will use this book to strengthen Christians and give them a closer walk with Him and to help many find Jesus as their Saviour.

May God continue to use Jack's ministry in reaching others for our Lord.

– Mrs. C. M. Hyles
May 1965

CHAPTER 1

Dost thou understand me, sinful soul? He wrestled with justice, that thou mightest have rest; He wept and mourned, that thou mightest laugh and rejoice; He was betrayed, that thou mightest go free; was apprehended, that thou mightest live; He wore a crown of thorns, that thou mightest wear a crown of glory; and was nailed to the Cross, with His arms open wide, to show with what freeness all His merits shall be bestowed on the coming soul; and how heartily He will receive it into His bosom?

– John Bunyan

Kisses of Calvary

"Mercy and truth are met together; righteousness and peace have kissed each other." (Psalm 85:10)

"Now he that betrayed him gave them a sign, saying, Whomsoever I shall kiss, that same is he: hold him fast. And forthwith he came to Jesus, and said, Hail, master; and kissed him."
(Matthew 26:48, 49)

"Kiss the Son, lest he be angry, and ye perish from the way, when his wrath is kindled but a little. Blessed are all they that put their trust in him." (Psalm 2:12)

One of the most beautiful statements in all of the Bible is the one I read a while ago, *"…righteousness and peace have kissed each other."* A dozen more sermons on the same Scripture are boiling up inside me.

One of the most beautiful romances in the world is the romance between righteousness and truth. They had been separated for 4,000 years, and when they got back together, they had to kiss. What a reunion!

A kiss is a very interesting thing. You will agree with that! I have always loved to kiss under proper conditions and proper people. A kiss of affection between members of the family certainly is good, and I would advise every family to teach boys and girls the expressiveness of kissing their mothers and fathers. Why, when I was a boy I never went out to play without kissing my mother goodbye. I never came home from the ball diamond without kissing Mother again.

In the Bible a kiss is certainly an interesting study. In Exodus 4:27, when Moses and Aaron met each other in the wilderness, they came to the mount of the Lord, and there they kissed each other.

I Samuel 10:1 says when Samuel came to anoint Saul as the first king of the people of God, that he anointed Saul with oil; then he kissed him.

When David and Jonathan, the sweetest friends in the Bible, humanly speaking, had been united after separation for a lengthy period, the Bible says that David and Jonathan kissed each other.

Joseph had been away from his brothers in Egypt for many, many long years. When his brothers came to him, he, unknown by them, provided provisions for their lives; then came that glorious day when Joseph revealed himself to his brothers. The Bible says that Joseph kissed his father and his brothers.

Esau and Jacob had come to the place of reconciliation. Esau had forgiven the trickster Jacob for having cheated him out of his birthright and out of the blessing of his father Isaac. When Jacob and Esau were united again, the Bible says there they kissed.

When Mary of Bethany anointed Jesus' feet, the Bible says that she kissed Him on the feet.

When Paul left the city of Ephesus in Acts, chapter 20, the Bible says the people clave unto Paul, they loved him so dearly . He had been their pastor for three glorious, wonderful years, but he longed to go back to Jerusalem, so he resigned his pastorate there. The Bible says they clave to him. They threw themselves on his neck and kissed him goodbye.

When the prodigal son returned from the far country and when he had spent all, his father *"kissed him"* and said, *"...put a ring on his hand, and shoes on his feet: And bring hither the fatted calf, and kill it; and let us eat...."*

In writing to the church at Corinth, the Apostle Paul said, *"Greet ye one another with an holy kiss."* In writing the church at Rome, the apostle admonished that they greet *"one another with an holy kiss."* Again in writing to the church at Thessalonica, the apostle admonished these people to greet one another in the services with an holy kiss.

Now bear in mind what that instruction means. In those days when you came in and sat down by somebody in church you kissed him. Now wait a minute. Don't do it—yet! There was also another difference in those days. In the early church the men and boys sat on one side, the ladies and girls on the other. Like we shake hands, they kissed each other. The men would kiss the men; the ladies would kiss the ladies. It was a sign of affection, a sign of fellowship, a sign of tenderness, a sign of love when you greeted one another with an holy kiss.

In I Peter 5:14, Peter speaks about greeting *"one another with a kiss of charity."*

I have enumerated at least ten places or more in the Bible where kissing was acceptable. But on the Cross of Calvary, there were three kisses: the kiss of reconciliation, the kiss of hypocrisy, and the kiss of salvation. As we approach the subject of kissing, we think of romance between a husband and wife, or the love between a mother and a son or daughter, or the love between a father and his son or daughter, or the love between brothers and sisters. My only sister and I always kiss hello and goodbye. When we say goodbye, there is weeping and tender words of expression of love, but we always kiss.

One of the saddest things about the age and area in which we live is the seeming belief that kissing and affection is a sign of emotional instability and weakness. It is not a sign of that, but our not wanting to kiss or otherwise to show affection is a sign of deadness and hardness and the fact that we are ashamed to express our feelings one to the other. Certainly there should be in the heart of every Christian a feeling of closeness, affection, and tenderness.

People across the country have often asked me, "How about the North and the South?" The South has a reputation of being wild and woolly, and they don't feel much. The North has the reputation of feeling it deeply and not saying much about it. All over the nation they say, "You have pastored in Texas and in Indiana—what do you think about it? Do you think the Southerner says it and doesn't feel it, and the Northerner feels it and doesn't say it?"

No, no, I don't think so. I have noticed Northerners when they sit on a tack, and I have noticed Southerners when they sit on a tack. A

Northerner jumps just as high when he is stimulated properly as the Southerner! Don't hide behind your geographical location for your coldness of heart and deadness of soul and the fact that you don't express love. Actually, people who love express it. People who feel it say so. People who are stimulated properly also respond properly.

Now let us notice the three kisses of Calvary. Two of them are beautiful, one of them tragic.

The Kiss of Reconciliation

Psalm 85:10 says, *"Mercy and truth are met together; righteousness and peace have kissed each other."*

When did righteousness and peace kiss each other? When did this wonderful reunion take place? When did righteousness see peace and peace see righteousness? When did they embrace and kiss? Truth came up from the ground, and righteousness looked down from Heaven, and there righteousness and peace met each other, and in a tender moment of embrace, they kissed. Righteousness or truth and mercy have kissed each other.

Peace and righteousness have walked together for many millenniums. In Heaven, peace and righteousness walk together. Oh, what a blessed walk it was for perfect peace between God and His creatures and perfect righteousness to walk together! There was no sin in Heaven.

Let me say this: the degree that you have of sin is also the degree you have of unrest and lack of peace. If you live righteously, you have more peace, and the more righteous you become, the more peace you will have.

And so in eternity peace and righteousness walk together. In Heaven with the angels they were such close friends. Peace was never without righteousness, and righteousness was never without peace. God made man. He put him in the Garden of Eden, and once again in the Garden of Eden peace walked hand in hand with righteousness. Righteousness was there. Peace was there. Adam and Eve were without sin. There was no sin originally in the Garden of Eden, and because there was no sin, there was peace. And so hand in hand, oh, the sweet fellowship that peace and righteousness enjoy! They loved each other, they walked together, and it was always a wonderful relationship.

But the day came when our lovers were forced to part. The day came when peace and righteousness divorced. The day came when peace and righteousness no longer could go with each other. Why was that? Sin came into the Garden of Eden. When sin comes, peace must leave. When righteousness is sinned against, then peace can stay no longer.

The reason you don't have peace in your home, you don't have righteousness in your home. You are not going to build a home with liquor in the ice box and sexy magazines in the magazine rack and the Beatles on your record player and fussing and cursing and lying and cheating and immorality. You are not going to build a home like that and have peace.

People all the time come to me and say, "Brother Hyles, our home has no peace. We can't get along. Our children are at each other. My wife and I can't get along. What is the trouble?" And in every case it is one word—SIN. When you get the righteousness problem settled, peace will go with righteousness. But when righteousness leaves, peace cannot stay any longer.

And so in the Garden of Eden the Serpent, Satan, came and said to Adam and Eve, "If you will eat this fruit, you shall live and be as God. Oh, I know God has said you will surely die, but if you eat this fruit, your eyes will then be opened. You don't know what you have had until you have had a fling with sin. You don't know what joy you can have until you do what I say."

The Devil always says that. The Devil always comes to young people and says, "You don't know what you are missing until you take a fling in sin." I'll tell you what you are missing when you are not in sin. You are only missing brokenness and heartfelt weakness and sadness and misery and unhappiness and unrest. Always when you go into sin, you leave peace. And so in the Garden of Eden, Adam and Eve reached out and took the forbidden fruit. Eve took the forbidden fruit; then she took it home to Adam. Now if Eve had been home baking biscuits, she wouldn't have seen the Devil in the first place. If Eve had been home sweeping the floor where she ought to have been—but no, Adam was probably home washing the dishes!

Did you hear about the henpecked husband? He went to the doctor and said, "Doctor, I'm henpecked."

"Well, what is the matter?"

"I have to cook all the time at home," the husband replied.

The doctor said, "Well, why did you come to me?"

He answered, "I had the most horrible dream."

When the doctor asked what his dream was, he said, "I dreamed I was on a boat with 12 gorgeous girls."

"Oh," the doctor said, "what is so bad about that?"

"Cooking for twelve people!"

Adam was home cooking some hot rolls and washing the breakfast dishes. Eve was out in the garden when she should have been home taking care of the household, and Satan tempted her. She took the fruit, she brought it back to Adam, Adam ate the fruit, and for the first time man had sinned against God. When man sinned, righteousness and peace could no longer walk together.

Now any time righteousness and peace must go, peace is the one that should go. It is better to have no peace and be right than have peace and be wrong. I am sick at my soul of politicians talking about appeasing Russia and appeasing communism and people co-existing. You can't be in the same room with a rattlesnake and have peace or coexistence. What happens? We have gotten to the place where we would rather have peace than righteousness. We are not willing to fight for truth any more. We are raising a soft, mealy-mouthed, shallow generation. We would rather be Red than dead. God give us some people who would rather be right and have war, than be wrong and have peace.

Oh, the greatest thing in this world is righteousness! And so when sin came in the Garden of Eden, peace and righteousness no longer could go with each other, and so peace left. For 4,000 years peace and righteousness were separated. Why? Sin had come. Righteousness could not accept peace. Peace wanted to come back but righteousness would not allow it. Peace could not come back to righteousness unless righteousness had been satisfied. Righteousness could not be satisfied unless payment for sin was made. So righteousness says sin must be paid for. Righteousness says sin must be condemned. Righteousness says no man can come to God unless the sin question has been settled.

So peace says, "Can I come back?"

And righteousness replied, "No. I want you back. I love you dearly. We walked together in Heaven. We walked together in Eden. I want you back, but I cannot receive you back, peace, until I have been satisfied."

What happened? God Himself came to the world in the form of a man. His name was Jesus Christ. For 33 long, lonely, homeless years Jesus lived a life of perfection and righteousness on the earth. Then at the end of those 33 years, Jesus Christ went to Calvary. On the Cross of Calvary the righteous One, Righteousness, was crucified. Righteousness took sin upon Himself, and Jesus died and He said, "It is finished." What He was saying was, righteousness has been satisfied, righteousness has been met; now peace can come home and, brother, you talk about a happy reunion!

Peace looked at righteousness and said, "Can I come back now?"

Righteousness answered, "Yes, you can. I have been satisfied now. The payment has been made. Jesus has died for the sins of the world." The sins of all the world were laid upon Him. Righteousness said, "Peace, won't you come back?"

Peace exclaimed, "Would I!" Peace looked up from earth and came out of the earth (that is the resurrection of Christ), and righteousness looked down from Heaven (that is the holiness and justness of God the Father), and peace and righteousness ran and threw arms around the cross of Calvary, and at Calvary they hugged and they kissed.

Now after 4,000 years those lovers had been reunited. That, dear friends, is the kiss of Calvary. God's justice has been satisfied. God's holiness has been met. In Jesus Christ and in Him alone can peace and righteousness walk together.

Do you want peace? Peace in your heart? Are you tired of tranquilizers? Of psychiatrists? Of misery? Are you tired of worry? Of fretting? Then come to Calvary. At Calvary righteousness and peace kissed each other and were reunited.

Ah, these reunions! I recall when my first furlough came when I was away in service. My mother and I had been close. Just the two of us lived together. Daddy was gone, my sister was married, and I was all that Mother had. I was all she had, and I had enlisted in the service. The first furlough came. I rode the streetcar and got off the streetcar at Bryant and San Jacinto Streets in Dallas, Texas. We lived about a block and two houses from the streetcar line; I looked down the street and saw my little mother up on her tiptoes looking to see if I had gotten off the streetcar.

When she saw those paratroopers walking down the steps of the streetcar, she took off running. She ran as fast as she could. I had run ten miles a day in the paratroopers, and I was as slim and trim as I am fat and sassy now, and I ran as fast as I could. I had done 90 push-ups with a field pack on my back, and I was as hard as rocks; yet my little old mother met me more than half way. Ah, she was glad to see me!

She took me home. "Son, this furniture—put it back where it was when you left. Son, I've got your favorite meal cooked." In those days it was veal cutlets, green beans, sauerkraut, thickened gravy, and biscuits. Ah, you can't beat that! Glory to God—that's eatin'! There it was on the table. We sat in our little kitchen in our little apartment and ate the food.

When it came time to go to bed, there was sweetness, tenderness, caresses, and kissing. Why? Because her boy had come home.

Oh. you talk about joy! For 4,000 years peace and righteousness had walked apart; for 4,000 years righteousness could not receive peace back because righteousness had not been satisfied. Then when one day on the Cross Jesus said, "It is finished." Once again righteousness said. "Hallelujah! Peace can return!" Peace came to righteousness, and on the Cross, they kissed. Once again, thank God, man can have peace because Christ has become his righteousness. They are together, and they have kissed. Now man can come himself and do some kissing at Calvary.

The Kiss of Hypocrisy

Not only was there a kiss of reconciliation when righteousness kissed peace, but the second kiss of Calvary was the kiss of hypocrisy. Judas Iscariot was watching, like the serpent he was, in the Garden of Gethsemane with the soldiers. Jesus was praying in the garden. *"…O my Father, if it be possible, let this cup pass from me: nevertheless not as I will, but as thou wilt."* As Jesus was saying this great prayer recorded in Mathew 26:39, He was overlooking the city of Jerusalem. He is in the Garden of Gethsemane, and Judas lurks outside the garden.

Judas tells the soldiers, "I'll show you the one by kissing Him. When I kiss Him, come and get Him." Judas Iscariot went out, and while our Lord was in Gethsemane, Judas did the most dastardly act ever done by human hands or lips—he placed the loving tenderness of a kiss on the brow of the Saviour. Upon doing so, the motley crowd of soldiers came and led Jesus away to be crucified.

Judas was kissing Jesus, but Judas made one mistake. He should have kissed Jesus. It was right to kiss Christ. Psalm 2:12 says, *"Kiss the Son, lest he be angry.…"* We are commanded to kiss Jesus Christ. That means kiss the feet of the Son; come and throw yourself at His feet and kiss Him. Man has been commanded to kiss the Son, BUT man cannot kiss the Son until righteousness and peace have kissed each other.

Judas made the mistake of kissing the Son without the meaning of Calvary. He kissed the Son short of Calvary. If that day when Jesus was on the Cross—lonely, forsaken, betrayed, suffering, crucified, deserted by man and God the Father—if Judas had come up then and meant it and thrown himself at the feet of the crucified One and kissed the kiss of affection and faith and trust, he could have been saved. But Judas made the mistake of kissing Jesus without reference to trust in Calvary. His was the kiss of hypocrisy.

Maybe you have made an effort to kiss Jesus. Maybe you have gotten religion. Maybe you have joined the church. But if you have kissed anything—I don't care what it is—and are trusting in anything short of Calvary, then you are a kisser of hypocrisy. There is nothing short of Calvary that can save you. The mistake that Judas made was kissing Jesus short of Calvary.

That is the reason that joining a church can't save anyone. That is a kiss short of Calvary.

That is the reason why living a good life, being a good friend, being a good spouse, and being a good neighbor can't save you. That is a kiss short of Calvary.

When you are sprinkled as a baby and they say that conveys some kind of mysterious salvation to you—I'm sorry, but that sprinkling won't take you one step toward Heaven. That is a kiss short of Calvary.

Being confirmed as a 12-year-old and learning the catechism of the church when you have never received Christ in believing faith won't take you to Heaven. That is a kiss short of Calvary.

Going into the baptistery and being baptized won't save you. That is a kiss short of Calvary.

When you go into a little room and confess your sins to a man (which is a waste of your time and his, as well as your money), that is why it doesn't do any good. You are kissing short of Calvary.

Coming and taking the holy communion and trusting that little wafer and that juice to save your soul won't do it. It is a kiss short of Calvary.

Joining the church as the result of a Baptist revival won't take you to Heaven. It is a kiss short of Calvary.

All the good deeds and the good works—anything that you do religiously won't take you to Heaven. It is a kiss short of Calvary.

The mistake Judas made was to kiss the Saviour short of Calvary. And to this day, Judas still resides in Hell, still burns in Hell, and still suffers the pangs of Hell. Why? He kissed the Saviour short of Calvary. Judas is in Hell because he didn't kiss Jesus at Calvary. Judas was a church member, yet he is in Hell because he trusted something short of Calvary. Judas was a preacher, yet he is in Hell because he trusted something short of Calvary. Judas was an apostle, but he is in Hell because he trusted something short of Calvary. Judas followed Jesus, but he is in Hell because he trusted something short of Calvary.

"Preacher, my church believes…" I wouldn't give you a dime for what your church or mine believes! The only thing that matters is that you can only kiss the Son at Calvary. The only place you can kiss the Son is at Calvary. Anything short of Calvary is a kiss of hypocrisy, and you will end up in Hell—thinking you were going to Heaven.

The Kiss of Salvation

The first kiss was when righteousness and peace kissed—the kiss of reconciliation. The second kiss was when Judas placed the kiss of betrayal and hypocrisy on the Saviour. The third kiss is the kiss of salvation. Psalm 2: 12 says, "Kiss the Son, lest he be angry, and ye perish from the way, when his wrath is kindled but a little. Blessed are all they that put their trust in him." Thank God for the third kiss—the kiss of salvation!

Jesus is dying. He speaks about it in the Psalms. His apostles have forsaken Him and fled. His followers are scattered. His Father looked on Him, saw Him in sin, and turned His back on the Son. Jesus hangs on Calvary, and the Psalmist said, "When righteousness and peace had kissed, then any poor sinner may come to Calvary; kiss the Son, and kiss His feet." What does that mean? It means the kiss of trust, the kiss of faith, the kiss of committal.

The verse begins, *"Kiss the Son, lest he be angry.…"* When you have not put your faith in Christ, it angers God. When you reject Jesus as your Saviour, it angers God. When a person says "no" to Calvary, God is angry, and His wrath is kindled. But the verse continues, *"…Blessed are all they that put their trust in him."* Blessed are those who have kissed the Son!

You are in one of these two groups: either you have kissed Him short of Calvary, or you have kissed Him at Calvary. Whether you kissed Him short of Calvary or at Calvary determines where you spend eternity. If you have kissed Jesus short of Calvary, if you have joined the church but have not been born again, you are lost. If you have been baptized short of Calvary, you are lost. If you have taken communion or sacraments or the Eucharist short of Calvary, you are lost.

If you have ever in your life come to Jesus Christ, seen Him crucified at Calvary, and heard Him say, "My God, my God, why hast thou forsaken me?…It is finished," then you know righteousness looked from Heaven, peace looked from earth, and they ran to each other, embraced, and kissed.

Righteousness said, "I'm satisfied! Now we can come back together." If you have ever seen that picture and have come to Jesus Christ in believing faith and said, "Dear Lord, I trust You. I kiss the Son. I believe in the Son," then God said He will take you to Heaven when you die.

Are you kissing short of Calvary this morning? Are you kissing short of Calvary? Let me illustrate: I am going to confess something that breaks my heart. I am going to confess something that will classify me as an awful, wretched sinner. Before I was married, I stole a couple of kisses from Mrs. Hyles! Isn't that awful? Those stolen kisses did not mean I was married. When the preacher said, "Wilt thou…," I willed it and said, "I will." When he said, "I now pronounce you as husband and wife," that kiss really meant something. Why? We had satisfied the laws of the land.

You can kiss the Son, but unless you have come and committed your life to Jesus Christ, as I gave my life to Beverly Slaughter and she became Beverly Hyles, all the religion and kissing you have done is not worth a dime. It is faith in Jesus Christ.

I thank God for that day when I looked up at Him and said, "Oh, God, I in faith receive Christ," and I kissed the Son, and I have been blessed in these years, for the Bible says in Psalm 2:12, "…*Blessed are all they that put their trust in him.*"

Have you trusted Him? If you died this morning, would you go to Heaven? Do you know you have put your faith in Him? Have you kissed the Son? Are you trusting Christ in Calvary? Have you trusted something short of Calvary? If you have, come to the Cross, see Him die, see peace and righteousness embracing and kissing. Kiss the Son, and you become a child of God.

CHAPTER 2

THE JUST
JUSTIFIER

A chaplain was speaking to a soldier on a cot in a hospital. "You have lost an arm in the great cause," he said.

"No," said the soldier with a smile. "I didn't lose it— I gave it."

In that same way, Jesus did not lose His life. He gave it purposefully."

– Anonymous

The Just Justifier

*(Preached at First Baptist Church, Hammond, Indiana
March 15, 1964 • Mechanically Recorded)*

Why did God make man? Why did God let man sin in the Garden of Eden? These and other questions I hope to answer. *"...that he might be just, and the justifier of him which believeth in Jesus."* (Romans 3:26)

Near the end of the Civil War, it is said that Abraham Lincoln took a tombstone to a typical grave of a soldier and placed the tombstone on the grave with the words: "My Substitute." This particular body and grave represented all the others who had died in the Civil War.

Christian, may I take you to our tombstone on which we would engrave the words: "Our Substitute"? I take you to Calvary, a little hill on the northern side of Jerusalem, just outside the city walls—a conspicuous spot. Nearby runs a highway. This place is called in the Bible the place of the skull, perhaps because the little hill is shaped like a skull. Others have advanced the possibility that it was called the place of a skull because it was the place where many had died, and their bones lay around the foot of the Cross. Whatever the purpose was, it was called Calvary, which means "the place of a skull."

The streams of ancient history all end at Calvary, and the beginning of all the rivers of modern history starts at Calvary. The eyes of Old Testament days looked toward Calvary; the eyes of modern civilization look back to Calvary. Calvary is the hub of the world. Geographically, it is in the center of the world. Theologically, it is in the center of all Christian preaching and religion.

Think for a minute. How many people on the Lord's day think of

Calvary? I suspect that more people think of Calvary than any other single subject on the Lord's day during the preaching hour. Truly Calvary is the hub of history, the hub of our speaking; Calvary is the center of poetry, art, sculpture, and religion. Calvary—authors have tried to pen the beauty of this word:

Years I spent in vanity and pride,
Caring not my Lord was crucified,
Knowing not it was for me He died
On Calvary.

Still another wrote:

There is a fountain filled with blood
Drawn from Immanuel's veins;
And sinners, plunged beneath that flood,
Lose all their guilty stains.

Another said:

On a hill far away stood an old rugged cross,
The emblem of suff'ring and shame.

The most popular song ever written leads the Gospel hit parade and has for many, many years: "The Old Rugged Cross." Said the author,

Oh, that old rugged cross so despised by the world,
Has a wondrous attraction for me.

So Calvary is the center of history. What is so important about Calvary? A Man died! Men have died before. A Man died on a Cross! Thousands have died on a cross before. What is so important about Calvary?

The liberals say He died to show us how to die. The modernists say He died as our example. No, they miss the hub entirely. What is the purpose of Calvary? What is it all about? I want to answer or attempt to answer this question by answering five other questions that are very basic and then explore the purpose of Calvary.

Why Did God Make Man?

The first question is, why did God make man in the first place? What is it all about? Did you ever wonder why you are here? Do you ever wonder why God made men such as we? Why did God make man?

The answer is very simple. God made man to fellowship with Himself. This is so important, yet we miss it. God is like us! People oftentimes wonder, "What is God like?" The answer is very simple. God is like us, except that He is not sinful. But in the nature of God, the attributes of God, and the personality of God, He is like us because the Bible said that man was made in the image of God. If God is like us, He is a God of emotions. He is a God of anger, a God of love, a God of compassion, a God who desires fellowship. Who among us wants to hermitize himself and live somewhere alone without fellowship with others?

So it was with God. God, being a God of love and fellowship, had a desire to fellowship with a creature. So God made Himself a race. From the dust He made Adam; from his rib made a woman, and God made them for fellowship with Himself.

The worst condition man can know is not to be loved. I cannot get away from the story about Charles Sumner who, on his deathbed, said the worst thing about it was that he had never heard anyone say, "I love you." None of us wants to live alone. All of us want fellowship. All of us want to be loved and want to love others.

So it was with Almighty God. God wanted the creation to love Him. Oh, He had the angels, but God wanted creation to love Him, so He made man in His own image so He could fellowship with man.

How many times have I said, if you are not in fellowship with God, you are not fulfilling the divine purpose for your life? God made you for Himself. You were not made to sin. You were not made for Satan. You were not made to go away from God. You were not made to stay home from church. You were not made to leave the Bible out of your life. You were not made to turn prayer away. You were made for God. You who do not fellowship with God and walk with God are living without fulfilling the ultimate purpose that every man was made for—fellowship with his Creator.

Why Did God Let Man Sin?

The second question I would ask leading up to the purpose of Calvary is why did God let man sin?

That question has been asked of me by thousands of people through the years. Many times I have had someone ask this question or one similar: "Preacher, I believe in God, but why would a loving and kind God let man go into sin?"

Let me make one statement quickly: God could have kept man from going into sin. God did not have to make man where he could sin. But God chose to make man where he could sin. Now, why would God do such a thing? The answer is very simple: God wanted someone to love Him, but He wanted man to choose to love Him. What if some discovery were made where a husband could take some serum, put it in a needle, and stick it in his wife's arm so she would have to love him? Not one husband would want that. He would not want his wife to wake up in the morning, act like a robot which mechanically says, "I-love-you. I-love-you. I-love-you." Every husband wants his wife to choose to love him.

God made a race because God is like us—He wants love. God does not want the love of someone who has no will. He made a race because God, the great heart of love; God, the great source of love; God, the great giver of love; God, the great lover, wanted to fellowship with that race and wanted someone to love Him. He could love like no one could love, and He wants to be loved like no one ever wanted to be loved.

God said, "I want my race to love Me because they want to love Me." So God gave us a choice to love Him or not to love Him. And man did love Him. Man loved Him, and man fellowshipped with Him. Oh, how happy that companionship made God!

On a typical Sunday morning, Mrs. Hyles and I drive separately to church. When we were preparing to leave she said, "Who is going with me?" (I always hope somebody will choose to go with me.) Becky said, "Mother, I will go with you."

Both Linda and Cindy said, "I'll go with you, Mother."

David said, "I want to go with Daddy." I didn't mind that a bit! Something in me wants to be loved!

Everybody wants to be loved. None of us get too much loving. We are made in the image of God, and if we want loving, think how much God wants love. God gave us a choice.

How happy He was every day when Adam and Eve would fellowship with Him. The purpose for God's creation had been fulfilled. Adam and Eve were walking with God. Every day they had had fellowship. God would come and walk in the cool of the garden with Adam and Eve. How sweet was their fellowship! How wonderful was their union! God made man to love Him, and man did love Him. God made man to fellowship with Him, and man did fellowship with Him. How happy that made the loving heart of God! That was the purpose of creation. Then came sin.

Every morning God came to the garden where Adam was, and God would call, "Adam, Adam!"

Adam would answer, "Yes, Lord. Here I am. Eve, the morning has come; let us go talk with the Lord."

Oh, the sweetness of fellowship! We know a little bit about it. We have never seen it, yet we know what it is to fellowship in our hearts with our Creator, our Maker. God would talk; then Eve would talk; then Adam would talk.

Adam would say, "Lord, I love You today."

The Lord would say, "Adam, that is what I made you for. I love you, too."

And Eve would say, "God, I love you, too!"

Oh, the sweetness of fellowship as they enjoyed the fragrances and delicacies of Eden's garden!

But one day God came walking in the garden. "Good morning, Adam. Adam, it is the Lord." There was no answer. "Oh, Adam! Adam! It is the Lord." Still no answer came. Adam and Eve had hidden themselves behind the trees and had made a covering of fig leaves. The Lord said, "Adam, you sinned, didn't you? You listened to Satan, didn't you? You did wrong, didn't you?"

Oh, listen. God is like we are. Add all of the sorrow that a mother has had over a wayward son to all the broken hearts of the wives whose husbands have left them and broken fellowship to all the broken hearts of fathers whose sons have gone into sin to all the broken hearts of little children whose fathers and mothers have left them to all the brokenness of fellowship the world has ever known—and you barely come close to the broken heart of our Heavenly Father. He had made man to fellowship with Him. That is what it was all about. Man has broken the fellowship with God.

A husband loves his wife, but if she came to him and said, "I'm leaving; I'm running off; I'm not going to live with you any more; it is all over," that husband would have a heart that was broken and crushed because of that broken fellowship.

If a wife had a husband come to her and say, "I love another," and he went off to live with another, oh, the broken heart that his wife would feel because of broken fellowship.

Man is made in the image of God. If God can love greater than man can love, then cannot God's heart be broken? The fellowship was broken, and God was heartbroken. He was grieved because man had left Him. Think of the heart of God. The reason very God did not make man so he could not sin is that God wanted man to love Him.

If you are out of fellowship with God, if you are not a Christian, if you do not know that you are saved, and if you do not walk with God, you grieve the heart of the Heavenly Father such as no one has ever before been grieved because no one can love like God can love.

Why Did God Not Just Forgive Man's Sin?

God did make man for fellowship with Himself. God did let man sin. The third question, Why then did God just not forgive man's sin? Why didn't God say to Adam and Eve, "Come on back; you are forgiven. Let's restore our fellowship"? God could have done so. Oh, yes, God could have said, "Adam, come on back." God could have forgiven man without man's being condemned to Hell. Yes, God could just have said, "Adam, come on back." But wait. Why did God not just immediately say, "All is forgiven. Come on back, and fellowship is restored"? Because God is just, as well as the Justifier.

One of the divine laws of God is that sin must be punished by expulsion from God Himself. When Satan sinned in Heaven, God expelled him from Heaven. When the angels sinned with him, God expelled them from Heaven. God is a God Who is just, and God's justice demands that sin be punished.

For many years, the masthead of the Edinburgh Review in Edinburgh, Scotland, carried the following slogan: "The judge is condemned when the guilty is acquitted." If God had not punished Adam and Eve, He would not have been just, and He would not have kept His word of the divine law that *"The soul that sinneth, it shall die...."* (Ezekiel 18:20) God would have fallen from His throne. In order to be God, to be just, and to be a just Justifier, God, with a broken heart, had to condemn man. God didn't say, "Okay, Adam, I hate you. Go on to Hell." No! No! God loved Adam. God made him, and God wanted him. God's righteousness is so wonderful and His justice is so perfect that God had to demand that sin be paid for.

Why Didn't God Just Let Man Go to Hell?

Ask any mother for the answer to the fourth question. Ask any mother from whose body came her little baby—flesh of her flesh, blood of her blood, and bone of her bone. She nurses the baby before the baby can nurture itself. Ask any mother to what lengths she would go to reclaim any child of her own.

So God looked down at His creation, and His heart was broken. We must face this fact: God is like we are, and God loves. He loves like we love, but He loves so much greater than we love. God is heartbroken like we are heartbroken, and God wants fellowship. The purpose of all of it was a hungering God Who wanted a people for Himself. God saw His people in sin, and He said, "I have to demand a penalty for sin. I must demand a penalty for sin." God could have said right then, "Okay, I'll let man go to Hell." God could have said right then, "Okay, man had the choice, and he chose to sin…"

People often ask why does a loving God send anyone to Hell? God never did send anyone to Hell. God never sent a soul to Hell. If you burn in Hell, if you die without God, if you someday suffer the torments of the unredeemed and burn in Hell without God, don't blame God for it. God has done everything from Heaven's glory to earth's gory. He even said goodbye to His Son, sent Him to die on the Cross, and turned His back on His Son. God never sent anyone to Hell. And if one person goes to Hell, it will be because he looks at God's provision for salvation and tramples under his feet Jesus' precious blood and His plan. He marks his own pathway toward Hell.

God doesn't want anyone to go to Hell. God said, "I could send them all to Hell, but I don't want to. I love them. I made them. They are My creation. I recall how I used to fellowship with them as we walked in the Garden of Eden. I want that fellowship again. I miss the sweetness that I had with Adam. I miss the days with Eve. I miss the walks in Eden's garden. I miss the fellowship. I miss the 'I-love-you's' they used to give Me."

Then God said, "I'm not going to let them go to Hell. I'm going to give them a plan whereby they will not have to go to Hell." And that decision leads to the fifth question that begs to be answered.

What Did God Do to Keep Us From Hell?

Why did God make us? For fellowship. Why did God let us sin? He wanted to give us a choice to love Him. Why did God not just forgive us? He could not within His justice and His divine nature of righteousness. Why didn't God let us go to Hell? He loved us too much.

Then what did God do to save us? What He did is all summed up in Matthew 27. God let His Son go to earth and to Calvary. Dying on the Cross, hanging between Heaven and earth, Jesus looked up toward Heaven and cried, *"...Eli, Eli, lama sabachthani?..."* (Matthew 27:46)

The people watching said, "He is calling for Elijah. Elijah can't help Him."

No, Jesus was not crying for Elijah. He was crying, *"...My God, my God, why hast thou forsaken me?"* Now what was He doing? In those words He was fulfilling the purpose of Calvary.

Sin must be paid for by you or by an innocent substitute. The priest cannot save anyone because he is not an innocent substitute. Jack Hyles cannot save anyone because he is not an innocent substitute. The church cannot save anyone because the church is composed of people who need saving themselves. Every person must pay for his sins or a substitute who does not owe for sin, who is perfect and sinless must be found. This perfect substitute is found in Jesus Christ Himself. And when this substitute, the Lamb of God, was hanging on Calvary and said, *"Eli, Eli, lama sabachthani?"* or *"My God, my God, why hast thou forsaken me?"* He was doing four things.

1.   **He was bearing our sins.** God could never look upon sin and be God. Jesus Christ took your sin and my sin and paid the price in full. Jesus said, "Put your sin upon Me." All my sin was heaped upon Jesus. All the times you drank and cursed and swore and left God out of your life were heaped upon Jesus Christ.

God said, "Hear ye! Hear ye! The court is in session." Jesus Christ stood before His Father, and God said, "I see You, Jesus, My Son, as a sinner. I see You becoming sin." All of our sins were on Him. God hammers the gavel of eternal justice and says to His Son, "Guilty! Guilty!" And that guilt of sin meant separation from God. God turned His back on His Son, and His Son bore your sin and my sin.

Take your choice. Either you bear your own sin or let Jesus bear your sin. Either you stand before God today and God will pronounce judgment upon you, or accept by faith what Jesus did for you on Calvary.

One morning I was studying in my office in the basement of our house when my daughter Becky came running and said, "Daddy, come quick! The Jack Ruby trial in Dallas is on television."

I rushed upstairs to watch the trial. I have never seen any more drama than I watched in that courtroom in a building I had passed thousands of times. I watched a judge I myself had seen many times as well as a district attorney with whom I had conversed. When the jurors had reached their verdict, the judge returned to the bench, and the jurors returned to their seats. The judge was given the slip of paper on which the verdict of the jurors had been written. When he opened the paper, I said to Becky, "This is drama!"

That judge opened that paper and read, "We find Jack Ruby guilty and sentence him to death in the electric chair."

I thought of the pomp, the drama, the bigness of it all. My mind wandered out to that day when Jesus Christ shall stand before you, and you will stand before Him. If you are not a Christian, He will say, "Guilty," and the punishment will be eternal separation from God Almighty. Jesus took death for you on the Cross, and when He said, *"My God…why hast thou forsaken me?"* He was taking your sins and my sins and bearing them on the tree.

2.   **He was suffering separation from God for you.** When Adam and Eve sinned in the Garden of Eden, they paid for that sin by being separated from God. They ran from God. Sin can never stay in the presence of God. You don't pray because you don't stay in God's presence enough. When you sin, it separates from God. You don't come to church on Sunday night because sin makes you not want to come where God is. You don't read your Bible because sin separates from God.

God said, *"The soul that sinneth, it shall die…."* The price for sin is separation from God. When Jesus died on the Cross and said, *"My God, my God, why hast thou forsaken me?"* and God turned His back on Him, and Jesus was by Himself, without the Father, He was suffering your separation from God. Now you take your choice: either you put your faith in Christ and accept the provision of God or you yourself must be separated from God forever.

3.   **He was suffering your Hell.** Not that He actually went down into the Lake of Fire and suffered in Hell, but He suffered our Hell for us. I know that whatever Hell is, Jesus suffered it. I know that all the punishment of Hell, Jesus suffered as your Substitute.

Now you have a choice. Either you trust His suffering your Hell, or you goto Hell yourself. Mark it down, if you never bow your knee to God, if you never say, "Lord God, be merciful to me a sinner," and become a Christian by faith in Christ, if you do not accept His payment, you must pay for it yourself, and you must go to Hell forever and forever.

You say, "Brother Hyles, you are ruining the worship service." You have no right to worship God and turn your back upon His Son. Your worship is idolatry if you are not a Christian. You come to church on Sunday morning and want some smooth, aesthetic feeling. You want to have worship with God, yet you have never put your trust and faith in His Son. It's idolatry and heathenism. The only worshippers are those who worship Him in Spirit and in truth. Jesus Christ is the truth, and either you accept the payment that He paid when He dipped His own soul into Hell and suffered your Hell, or you will have to suffer it yourself. When Jesus said, *"Eli, Eli, lama sabachthani?"* He was suffering your separation from God and my separation from God. He was suffering your Hell, and He was suffering my Hell.

4.   **He was suffering the sum total of what every sinner would ever suffer in Hell.** All of it! Jack Hyles deserved to go to Hell. If I were to go to Hell, all the suffering that I would ever suffer in Hell was put on Jesus. All the suffering that Jim Lyons would ever suffer in Hell was put upon Jesus. And all the suffering that Charlie Hand would ever suffer in Hell was put upon Jesus. And there with all the sins of the world, God's Lamb, our Substitute, our Sacrifice, hung.

Bad enough to have the world laughing at Him. Bad enough to be hanging nude on the Cross. Bad enough to have nails and spikes in His hands and feet, a crown of thorns on His head. Bad enough to have them slapping Him and spitting in His face, and laughing and mocking and jeering, and plucking His eyebrows and His fingernails. It was bad enough, but oh, the Father was still there. And I think the Father, Who is a loving Father like we are, said, "Son, the time has come."

And the Son said, "It has to be done. All right, I'll do it. Thy will be done, not Mine."

And the Father said, "Son, I made a race thousands of years ago, and I love them. I made them to love Me. I made them to fellowship with Me, but they sinned. And Son, I'm just. I cannot let them come back unless they pay the price. And You are the only One Who is sinless that has ever walked the earth."

Then Jesus said to the Father, "Nevertheless, not My will, but Thine, be done." He followed, setting His face like a flint toward Calvary, and there He suffered the price that you and I deserved to suffer. He suffered our Hell. He bore our sins. He took our punishment. He became our Substitute.

Now He looks to us—His race whom He made and with whom He had fellowship. That race had fallen, and now He has redeemed that race. If we will come to God through Jesus Christ by faith, that fellowship can be restored, and for all of eternity we can know the communion that Adam and Eve had with God in the Garden of Eden.

May God help you to turn to Him Who alone is the just Justifier.

Chapter 3

The Fullness of the Spirit

Men are God's method. The church is looking for better methods; God is looking for better men. What the church needs today is not more machinery or better, not new organizations or more and novel methods, but men who the Holy Spirit can use—men of prayer, men mighty in prayer. The Holy Spirit does not come on machinery but on men. He does not anoint plans, but men—men of prayer.

– Edward McKendree Bounds

The Fullness of the Spirit

(Preached at the Fellowship of Evangelical Baptist Churches in Canada)

"And be not drunk with wine, wherein is excess; but be filled with the Spirit." (Ephesians 5:18)

If next Sunday morning the pastor of this church were to come to the platform and it was obvious to each member of this church that the pastor had been drinking alcohol and was inebriated, someone would stand to his feet and make a motion immediately that the pastor not fill the pulpit that day. The Bible is very plain about this matter. Ephesians 5:18 says very distinctly, *"...be not drunk with wine, wherein is excess...."*

If tonight when the song leader approached the platform to announce the opening hymn and he had a bleary, glassy look in his eyes, an unsure step, and a heavy leaning on the platform, and if those in the front row could smell alcohol on his breath, the moderator would have said, "I make a motion tonight that this song leader not be allowed to lead the singing in this meeting." The Bible is so plain about that. It says in Ephesians 5:18, *"...be not drunk with wine, wherein is excess...."*

If next Sunday morning in your church someone came to your pastor about 10:00 o'clock and relayed the news to him that a certain superintendent was drunk in his Sunday school department, no doubt your pastor would be horrified. The Bible is very plain about that. It says in Ephesians 5:18, *"...be not drunk with wine, wherein is excess...."*

If a deacon in your church drinks liquor and you find it out, you would (or at least you should) dismiss that deacon from the deacon board. The Bible is very plain. *"...be not drunk with wine, wherein is excess..."* says Ephesians 5:18.

If a Sunday school teacher came to church drunk Sunday morning, you would say, "You'll not teach the class this morning." The Bible is very plain in Ephesians 5:18, which says, *"...be not drunk with wine, wherein is excess...."*

My precious friends, there is something else to notice in Ephesians 5:18. Who am I to say that it is less important than the other? *"And be not drunk with wine, wherein is excess,"* and the dual command is, *"... but be filled with the Spirit."* If I understand the Bible, it would be an equal sin for the pastor of this church to come to the pulpit next Sunday not filled with the Spirit or if he came to the pulpit drunk with wine, wherein is excess. It would have been as much a sin for the song leader to come tonight not filled with the Spirit as it would have been for him to have come drunk with wine, wherein is excess. For a departmental superintendent or a teacher or a pastor or any officer of the church not to do his work in the anointing and energy of the Holy Spirit would be a sin equal to that of doing his work in the energy of alcohol—*"...drunk with wine, wherein is excess."*

The same verse in the same chapter in the same book in the same Bible gives the same emphasis to these two commands:

- Be not drunk with wine wherein is excess.
- Be filled with the Spirit.

I want to speak on the subject, "The Fullness of the Spirit." I beg your leniency and please do not crucify me as I address this subject. I was preaching on baptism recently in the state of Arkansas, and I overheard a fellow ask another person, "I wonder what his position on baptism is?"

I stopped to answer his question. "When somebody asks, 'What is your position on baptism?' I always answer, 'My position on baptism is this: I stand up straight and lower the person being baptized like this. That's my position.'"

By the way, I am a Baptist. I heard about a good Baptist lady who was in a Catholic hospital. The nun gave her a little doll and said, "When your pain gets excruciating, rub the doll and that will help."

"Oh, no," said she, "I am not a Catholic. I am a Baptist."

"Well," the nun said, "if you do find yourself in pain and get a little worried, rub the doll anyway."

"I won't rub this doll—I don't care how much pain I get in.

The nun said, "I'll leave it here just in case you change your mind."

About 2:00 o'clock in the morning, the little lady had the pain hit her, and she looked at the doll. "Oh, I couldn't do it. I am a Baptist," she said. Finally about 3:00 o'clock in the morning, an unbearable pain hit her. She reached for the doll, and with trembling hands she looked up to Heaven as she rubbed the doll, and said, "Dear Lord, don't let this crazy little doll fool You. I'm still a Baptist at heart!"

I am a Baptist, but I am a Baptist who believes in doing the work of God in the energy of the Holy Spirit. We are in desperate need of reflecting this blessed Person of the Trinity in our churches. I am afraid too often we have made Sunday morning God the Father's service and Sunday night God the Son's service. We dare not sing about Jesus on Sunday morning. We dare not witness of Jesus on Sunday morning. He is not dignified enough for the Sunday morning service, so we relegate Him as a second-rate Sunday night attraction. And I am more afraid that we have not put the Holy Spirit anywhere. Because some have perverted this blessed truth, we have left off the teaching of the Holy Spirit altogether.

Now tonight if you are a Pentecostal, I speak to you on the subject of "The Baptism of the Holy Ghost." If you are a Nazarene, I speak to you on "Sanctification." If you are a Wesleyan, I speak to you on "Perfect Love." If you are a Quaker, I speak to you on "Overcoming Power." If you are a Presbyterian, I speak to you on "Death to Self." If you are a Baptist, I want to speak on "What We Ain't Got That We Desperately Need in Our Churches"!

I am not talking about talking in tongues. I am not talking about getting sanctified. Whatever you believe it is—I'm talking about getting that power in your life and upon your ministry. As a kid preacher, I used to walk in the pine thickets of East Texas over those old sandhills and say, "Dear Lord, I read a book about this, and I want to talk in tongues." I would read another book, and I would say, "Lord, I want sanctification."

I would read yet another and say, "Lord, I want perfect love." I didn't get a thing.

Then one time I said, "Lord, I don't know what it is, I don't know all about it, I don't know all the theology—all I know is, I'm not going to have a powerless ministry. I'm not going to go to my pulpit Sunday after Sunday in the energy of the flesh. I am not going to settle for anything less than a supernatural enduement from Heaven." And when I quit worrying so much about the theological explanation and the practical acceptance of it, God gave me a little bit of that which I wanted.

Tonight we are utterly powerless and helpless unless we are living our ministry in the energy of the Holy Spirit. This doctrine of the fullness of the Spirit is a Bible truth. I like what Dr. Bob Jones, Sr., said:

> "I had rather a fellow say, 'I seen,' who has seen something, than say, 'I have seen,' when he ain't seen nothing."

And I would rather you be a little wrong and have power than to have all the *i's* dotted and all the *t's* crossed and not have the power of God.

I. It Is Bible Truth.

- In Acts 1:4 we read, *"wait for the promise of the Father."*
- In Acts 1:5 we find the words, *"baptized with the Holy Ghost."*
- In Acts 2:4 we find *"they were all filled with the Holy Ghost"*—fullness of the Spirit.
- Luke 24:49 says, *"...endued with power from on high"*—enduement of power.
- In Acts 1:8 we find the words, *"The Holy Ghost is come upon you."*
- In Acts 2:17 we find the pouring out of the Holy Spirit.
- In Luke 11:13 and also in Acts 2:38, 39, we find the gift of the Holy Spirit.
- In Ephesians 5:18 we find the expression, *"be filled with the Spirit."*

Whatever you care to call it, whatever you care to term it, whatever you believe about its teaching—whether you believe in a gradual process of being filled or whether you believe in one filling and that's all, or whether you believe, as I do, in many fillings over and over and over again—whatever you believe, I'm concerned tonight about your going home and getting on your face before God and saying, "O God, I will not be a powerless preacher. I will not be a powerless teacher. I will not be a powerless singer. I will not be a powerless Sunday school worker. I will not be a powerless deacon." I'm concerned about Baptist people getting the breath of God and divine unction upon their ministry.

I like what the old colored fellow said down in the South: "Lord, give me the unction. Give me the unction."

A fellow asked, "What is the unction?"

"I don't know what it is," he replied, "but I know what it ain't, and it sure is terrible without it."

"Lord, give me the unction"—that's what we need. We need something akin to Wesley when he walked with God. We need something akin to George Whitefield when he would come home with blood dripping down his face after he had walked with God and preached the Gospel. We need something akin to George Fox who stayed in a trance for 14 days. We need something akin to Savonarola who sat in his pulpit in a trance for five hours. We need something akin to David Brainerd who walked with God and left his kneeprints on the soil of the northwestern country praying for God to send revival. We need desperately a new anointing upon our lives and ministries in our Baptist churches.

Brother, if program would save the world, we would be in the millennium tonight. If plans and pulpits and copied sermons and homiletics and hermeneutics and apologetics and exegesis would bring in the kingdom, the wolf and the lamb would be lying down together tonight in the Holy Land. If our plans and programs, our education, our formality, our pomp, our depth would bring in the kingdom, we would be right in the midst of the kingdom tonight.

I'm saying that the program is no good unless it is anointed by the Holy Ghost. I'm saying the personality and pomp and all the rest of it is as sounding brass and a tinkling cymbal unless it has the holy breath of

God Almighty and unless our labor of love is done in the energy of the Holy Spirit of God.

Oh, to preach in His power! Oh, to preach when there is that sweet, fresh settling of heavenly dew upon the congregation! How awful it is to preach in the energy of the flesh. Stories fall flat, words fall flat, poems fall flat, illustrations fall flat—all because we preach in the energy of the flesh. O God, breathe upon us in these days and cause us to seek His power.

One of my favorite historical characters is Billy Bray, an old Cornish coal miner who got converted and shouted everywhere he went. Every time Billy Bray met someone, he would shout, "Hello! Amen! Hallelujah!" And if you didn't say, "Amen!" he would think you were not saved.

Somebody said, "Billy, don't talk like that. And you're singing all the time, and you can't carry a tune."

Billy said, "Hush! God would just as soon hear a crow as a nightingale. I'll sing all I want to sing."

"Billy," the person said, "shut your mouth."

"If I shut my mouth, my feet would still shout. Every time my left foot hits the ground, it says 'Amen!' And every time my right foot hits the ground, it says, 'Well, glory,' and I can't help myself."

Billy had the breath of heavenly dew upon him. He had this unction and anointing upon him. And from that moment forward, Billy Bray was aflame for God, walking up and down the streets witnessing, preaching whenever he had opportunity, testifying to all with whom he came in contact—because he was anointed with the Holy Spirit.

Somebody said to him, "Billy Bray, you're going to die."

He said, "You mean I'm dying now?"

"Yes."

"Glory to God! I'll be Home by morning!"

"Billy, what if you go to Hell? What if you had been mistaken all these years?"

"I'll just shout all the way to Hell. I'll say, 'Glory! It was wonderful to think I was going to Heaven all those years!' I'll just praise the Lord because I thought I was going to Heaven, and I had a wonderful life. If I go to Hell I'll say, 'Amen! Glory to God! What a wonderful life it was!' And if the Devil walks up and says, 'Billy, you can't shout like that here,' I will say, 'I've got to shout! It's in my bones!' And if the Devil will say, 'You've got to get out of here,' I'll say, 'That's what I'd like to do anyway, old Devil, if you don't mind.' And I'll just shout all the way to Glory! Praise the Lord! Glory to God! I'm saved!"

I'm not saying that everyone who shouts, "Praise the Lord!" has Holy Spirit power. I'm not saying that everybody who says, "Hallelujah" has the anointing. But I am saying that there needs to settle upon the Baptist churches and others a new breath of God that will give us joy and conviction and tears and something supernatural transpiring in our public services. It is a Bible truth.

II. It Is an Old Testament Truth

- Jacob in Genesis 32:26 wrestled with the angel and said, *"...I will not let thee go, except thou bless me."*
- Isaiah saw the seraphim take the coal from off the altar and place it upon his tongue, and he said, *"...Woe is me! for I am undone... ."* (Isaiah 6:5)
- Ezekiel wept in the bitterness of the Spirit.
- Elisha took Elijah's mantle and received a double portion of blessing.
- Judges 6:34, *"But the Spirit of the LORD came upon Gideon...."*
- I Samuel 11:6, *"And the Spirit of God came upon Saul...."*
- I Samuel 16:13, *"...the Spirit of the LORD came upon David...."*

How did Gideon win the battle over the Midianites with a few folks who lapped water like dogs? How did Gideon win the battle when he put the fleece out and God miraculously delivered the Israelites from the Midianites' power? How did David slay a lion? How did David kill a bear? How did David with a stone kill Goliath? How did Saul win his battle? How did Samson have his power? In the energy of the Holy Spirit!

This truth has been from the time that the Spirit of God moved upon the face of the water in Genesis 1, *"And God said, Let there be light: and there was light."* From that day until this, everything that has been done by God Almighty through God's men has been done in the energy and power of the Holy Spirit. If revival comes in your church, it will come when we cease to work and let Him work. As A. B. Simpson used to say:

> *Once* it was the blessing, now it is the Lord;
> Once it was a feeling, now it is His Word;
> Once His gifts I wanted, now the giver own;
> Once I sought for healing, now Himself alone.
> All in all is Jesus, of Jesus I will sing,
> Everything is Jesus and Jesus everything.

III. It Is a New Testament Truth

- John the Baptist said, *"...he shall baptize you with the Holy Ghost and with fire."* (Luke 3:16)
- Luke 4:1 says, *"...Jesus being full of the Holy Ghost...."*
- Acts 4:31 says, *"...they were all filled with the Holy Ghost."*

What I like about this is that the work Jesus did, He did in the energy of the Holy Spirit, as a man filled with the Spirit and not as God Himself. He wanted to be our example. He wanted to set a pattern for us. So the work that He did, He did in the same power that God uses to do the work in the First Baptist Church of Hammond every Sunday morning. The same power—the power of the Holy Spirit!

When Jesus preached to Zacchaeus up a tree, to the thief on the Cross beside Him, and to the woman beside the well, they were saved because He worked in the energy of the Holy Spirit. He did not perform a miracle, He never opened one blind eye or deaf ear as far as the Bible records, He never caused one lame person to leap with joy, one dumb person to speak, one dead person to live until He went into the baptismal water and was anointed with the power of the Holy Spirit of God.

When 32 people came to Christ on a recent Sunday morning in First Baptist Church of Hammond, five of them deaf but hearing the message through the deaf interpreter, it was done, bless God, in the same power that was used to save the little lady beside the well in Sychar. Think of it! Man has at his disposal the same blessed power that Jesus had—the energy of the Holy Spirit.

In Luke 11 a fellow comes to a friend's home at midnight and says, "Friend, wake up!"

The homeowner shakes himself, gets up, opens the window, and says, "Yes?"

"Say, a friend has come to me in his journey, and I have nothing to set before him to eat. I really need three loaves of bread. May I please borrow them?"

"Come back in the morning. We're all sleeping now. Come back in the morning." He puts down the window and goes back to bed.

This fellow starts home, but he decides he can't go home. "I have a friend who needs bread. I can't holler back up there, but I can't go home either. My friend is hungry. I must have the bread."

Again he calls, "Friend! Friend!"

The friend wakes up, his wife wakes up, Johnny wakes up, Sue wakes up. He raises the window, "YES?"

"Friend, I know it's going to make you angry, and I hate to bother you, but a friend of mine in his journey has come to me, and I have nothing to set before him."

"I told you to come back in the morning. I'm trying to sleep. My family is in bed." Again he slams the window shut.

The fellow starts home. "I can't go home. My friend is waiting. He's expecting me to return with some food. I'm going to go back—I can't go back. That fellow would kill me. But I'm going to do it. No, I can't do it. I'm going to go home, but I can't go home."

(That reminds me of a preacher on Sunday morning with people sitting before him, and he has nothing to set before them. The people say, "Give us three loaves. We're hungry." Many times the preacher goes to his sermon outline books and his homiletics books. He goes down deep and stays down long and comes up dry, and the folks stay hungry. Oh, we need to go to God all week long, day after day and say, "O God, lend me three loaves for the students in my Sunday school class, or for the members of my church, or for my department. They have come to me, and I have nothing to set before them.")

The fellow trudges back and cries again, "Friend?"

His friend wakes up. His wife wakes up. Johnny wakes up. Sue wakes up. He raises the window, "YES?"

"Friend, I cannot go home. I know you are angry at me, but I must have some bread."

"If you will not bother me any more while I sleep, I'll give you a bakery. Just go home and leave me alone." And so he finally gives him the three loaves.

The teaching is this: he would not give it to him merely because he asked him; rather, he gave it to him because of his importunity. The word importunity means "much asking, begging." God give us a ministry where we'll know what it is to ask God for Sunday morning. May God give us churches in Canada, in every state, and around the world, that have preachers come before them on Sunday with warm bread they just got from Heaven's bakery!

I have often read of the life of Bud Robinson, a Nazarene preacher. He believed in sinless perfection. He was wrong in his doctrine, but he came far closer to being sinlessly perfect than I do! In one of his sermons he tells this story:

> Ladies and gentlemen, I was in the hospital in Atlanta, Georgia, and the "holy father" came to my room. The priest said to a fellow on the side of me, "Is there anything you want to confess to me?" Oh, I have never heard such language as that man done confessed.

> Then he went to the fellow on the other side and said, "Are there any sins you want to confess to me?" Oh, I had to shut my ears, that man was confessing so many wicked sins.

> Then the "holy father" came to me, a born-again Christian, and said, "Uncle Bud, any sins you want to confess to me?"

> And I said to the "holy father," "Put your ear down as close to my mouth as you can get. I would like to confess just one thing to you."

> And the "holy father" put his ear right down close to my mouth, and he said, "All right. Confess."

> When the "holy father" put his ear right on my mouth, I

opened my mouth good and wide and shouted, **"Glory to God! I'm saved and sanctified and full of the Holy Ghost and on my way to Glory!"** The last time I saw the "holy father," he was running down the hall!

Brother, let us all make up our minds that we are not going to fight the battles of Catholicism, Modernism, New Evangelicalism, Neo-orthodoxy, Liberalism, etc., without the anointing of the Holy Ghost upon our ministry. I trust some preacher will go home from this meeting, get out by himself and say, "By God's grace I am going to spend less time doing the little things and do the big things for God. I'm going to pray, I'm going to pray, I'm going to PRAY."

I was in Phoenix, Arizona, preaching a sermon on the power of God, and I said, "Why don't you pray constantly for God's power?" I was pricked with conviction. I said to myself, "You don't pray constantly for God's power." That was a year ago. I promised God before I left that service that night that I would spend every conscious waking moment when I was alone asking Him for His power. I'll say I have not kept that promise totally, but I will say I started praying driving down the highway. "O God, give me power." On the airplane I say, "O Lord, give me power. Lord, give me power." Before I preach I say, "Lord, give me power. Oh, give me the power of the Holy Spirit." I have seen a tremendous change in the blessings of God upon my life.

God help us. Too many Christians are so afraid somebody is going to call them fanatical—and it might be one of the biggest compliments they ever had.

Peter was filled with the Holy Spirit on Pentecost. In Acts 9:17, Paul was filled with the Holy Spirit. From the time the Holy Spirit breathed upon the waters in Genesis 1 till this good hour, it has always been through the energy of the Holy Spirit that God does His work.

IV. It Is an Historic Truth

Not only is it an Old Testament truth and a New Testament truth, but it is also an historic truth.

We love to speak about the great men. Oh, how I love to walk with them in their lives. We refer often to men like George Whitefield and Dwight L. Moody, and Billy Sunday. I am reminded that every time Billy Sunday preached a sermon, he opened to Isaiah 61:1, which says, *"The Spirit of the Lord GOD is upon me...."*

For centuries this teaching of the anointing of the Holy Spirit with supernatural power was as common as Sunday school talk is today. Savonarola prayed in a trance for five hours in his pulpit, and God's power came upon him.

George Fox, burdened about his sins and powerlessness, went to a priest and said, "What should I do?"

The priest answered, "You should get married."

Another advised, "You ought to join the Army."

Still another priest said, "You ought to try tobacco and hymns."

George Fox went alone and fasted and prayed for 14 days. (Let me stop to say this. This matter of fasting oftentimes is not a ritualistic thing. If we want to have the breath of God upon us, sometimes we must forego the conveniences and pleasures of the world.) George Fox stayed in a trance for 14 days, and the power of God came upon his life.

On October 3, 1730, John Wesley, George White field, and 60 other preachers prayed all night. At 3:00 o'clock in the morning John Wesley said, "There has come upon me the blessing of God, and for the first time I know what it is to be filled with the Holy Spirit."

All day June 20, 1736, before his ordination service, George White-field had a feeling he should not be ordained without the power of the Holy Spirit upon his life. He said, "I'll not be a preacher unless God gives me the power of the Holy Spirit." Later he said, "On my knees that night when Bishop Benson laid his hand upon my head, there was such a yielding to God's blessed will for my life that then and there I knew for the first time that by faith I had been filled with the Holy Spirit."

While in an eastern city, Dwight L. Moody was overcome with the power of God, for which he had prayed so long. One day the power came upon him while he was on the street, and he had to go to an upstairs room of a dear friend and say, "Lord, withhold Your power till I can get alone with You."

George Mueller was in the house of friends. He saw Christians on their knees for the first time. George Mueller was so impressed about seeing Christians praying on their knees, he said, "I am going to go alone and pray on my knees." And on his knees he went, and the Holy Spirit's power came upon him.

Charles G. Finney said the night he was converted the Holy Spirit's power came upon him for soul winning. Peter Cartwright said when he preached his first sermon in Atlanta, Georgia, the Holy Spirit's power came upon him.

Christmas Evans was riding his circuit on horseback. That old one-eyed preacher, whose eye was put out from witnessing the first day he was converted by the same crowd he had gone with in the world, got off his horse and fell on his face. He said, "Lord, I can't be a powerless preacher any more." Such power came upon him that he was never the same again. As old Christmas Evans died, preachers gathered around him and said, "Mr. Evans, what can you say for us on your deathbed?"

He said, "Young men, preach the blood in the basin. Preach the blood in the basin."

That's our need, dear friends. New buildings? That's wonderful, but that's not the big need. Good sermons? That's wonderful, but that's not the big need. Organization? I believe in organization. If you read any of my books, you will find I believe in organization. But that's not the big need. Trained workers? Oh, yes, we ought to train our workers. We spend an hour and a half every week on Wednesday night training our workers. I believe in training, but that's not the big need. Good voices? Great delivery? That's wonderful, except that Jonathan Edwards read everything he ever preached, and his eyes were so bad he had to put the print right close to them. He read in a very weak voice—and the power of God came upon him. The power of God is the greatest need!

The greatest need we have in our Sunday school is for the anointing of the Holy Spirit. The greatest need we have for our churches is for the anointing of the Holy Spirit. The greatest need our ministry has is not polish nor dignity—it's for God's supernatural power to settle upon His people.

V. It Is a Twentieth Century Truth

The fullness of the Holy Spirit not only is an Old Testament truth, a New Testament truth, and an historic truth, but praise God, it's a twentieth century truth!

God knows I would never stand before you as an example. There are preachers here tonight who were preaching before I was born and were doing a better job before I was born than I am doing tonight. But let me say this: I would have to say that that which God has done through this simple little preacher must be in the power of the Holy Spirit.

I was an introverted boy—a poor, barefooted country kid with hand-me-down clothes when I trusted Jesus in the backyard of the Fernwood Baptist Church of Dallas, Texas. I was timid and cowed, with no ability, and I sucked my thumb until I was almost 14 years old! My first sermon lasted five minutes. I preached on Peter and petered out in five minutes. Then all of a sudden one day when I was in college, a professor came to me and asked, "Are you a preacher?"

I had been in school about one week, and I said, "That's a hard question to answer." (I had only preached five minutes.) But I added, "Yes, Sir, I am a preacher."

He said, "Would you preach for me next Sunday?"

Oh my! No outlines, no sermons, no illustrations—if I had had an illustration, I would not have had anything for it to illustrate. I didn't know a thing, but I said, "I'll do it."

My wife and I went out that Sunday morning to a little country church just south of Marshall, Texas. She was scared to death, and she had a right to be! Five minutes was all I had ever preached. I got up to preach. I preached five minutes, then ten minutes, then twenty minutes, and then thirty minutes! I could see Mrs. Hyles sitting in the audience with her mouth wide open, and I was thinking, "Can any good thing come out of this?" But I preached!

All of a sudden the blessing of God came on my soul, and I really felt that Someone was helping me besides myself. I was preaching. This little country preacher didn't know a verse, didn't know an illustration—didn't know a thing. I said, "This is the greatest thing in the world! Lord, to preach in the power of the Holy Spirit is the greatest thing in the world." When I finished, a fellow walked up to me and said, "Here is your check."

When I asked, "What for?" he said, "Twelve dollars."

"Not what for—what for? What for?"

When he said, "For preaching!" I said in wonderment, "You get paid for this?"

He said, "You sure do."

I said something to him I am so sorry I said. "I'll never take a dime for preaching the Gospel as long as I live." I've changed a little bit since I made that statement!

I want to say this: for God to take a country preacher like that and let him see people saved Sunday after Sunday—glory be to His name! In these blessed years I could count on the fingers of my right hand the Sundays that we have not had folks saved. My oldest girl Becky is 11 years old, and she has never lived a Sunday without seeing someone saved. Only two Sunday nights—God gets the praise for this—in 11 years has Becky not seen her daddy in the baptistery baptizing to close the day.

Oh, who could do that? Who could do that? Me? Not on your life. Was it my ability? Oh no! No! A thousand times no! Only the power of the Holy Spirit could do that, and you may have it!

I read last week about the Scottish revival and how all Scotland said, "Knox is coming! Knox is coming!" There was such power that there was preaching sometimes six and seven services even in Presbyterian churches on Sunday. I say, "Lord, do it again! Do it again!"

I read about the New Hebrides revival and how seven men prayed all night every Thursday night. One time these faithful seven got up from their knees about four o'clock in the morning and walked out to go to their homes. The lights were already on in the area. Vehicles had stopped beside the road. People had gotten out of their vehicles and were kneeling and confessing their sins. They saw lights all around the villages and heard people crying, confessing sin, and asking God to save them. Revival broke out. There were seven or eight services every Sunday in every church on the island. I say, "Lord, do it again!"

You know, my precious friend, that unless something happens, our generation will never see revival. Somebody told me that Canada has never seen revival—I don't know if that is true. But please tell me, if Canada sees revival, who will be responsible? You tonight must seek God's face.

Let's face it, brethren. Go home and look in the mirror. The hope for Canada is not in Ottawa or in London or in Washington. The hope for the nation and the world and the continent does not lie in guarding Cuba tonight, though I think it is a wise move. I say the hope lies in the burning bosom of Gospel preachers like you and like me, in a Bible-loving, Christ-honoring people.

May God help us not to be drunk with wine wherein is excess, but to be filled with the Spirit.

CHAPTER 4

THE DIGNITY OF MAN

When the poor heart is bleeding and the man is already suffering the very extremity of misery, who would wish to add a single ounce to the crushing weight he has to carry?

– Charles Haddon Spurgeon

The Dignity of Man

(Preached October 22, 1962,
at the Fellowship of Evangelical Baptist Churches in Toronto, Ontario, Canada)

*"When I consider thy heavens, the work of thy fingers, the moon
and the stars, which thou hast ordained; What is man, that thou
art mindful of him? and the son of man, that thou visitest him?
For thou hast made him a little lower than the angels, and hast
crowned him with glory and honour. Thou madest him to have
dominion over the works of thy hands; thou hast put all things
under his feet: All sheep and oxen, yea, and the beasts of the field;
The fowl of the air, and the fish of the sea, and whatsoever passeth
through the paths of the seas. O LORD our Lord, how excellent is
thy name in all the earth!"* (Psalm 8:3-9)

Several thousand years ago David looked up one night and saw the
stars. Perhaps he did not know that the earth was 8,000 miles in di-
ameter, containing 198,980,000 square miles. Perhaps he did not know
that there are 264,000,000,000 cubic miles on the earth, and even though
the earth is that size, Saturn is 995 times as large and Jupiter 1,281 times
as large. Perhaps he did not know that though the earth in all its immensity is so big, the sun could contain 1,384,462 earths. He looked up at the
stars as I have done so many times.

I am still childish enough to take an occasional walk and look at the
stars. "Star light, star bright, first star I've seen tonight; I wish I may, I
wish I might have the wish I wish tonight," I've quoted many times since
I was a little boy. Or, "Twinkle, twinkle, little star, how I wonder what

you are; up above the world so high like a diamond in the sky." I love the stars. There's a fancy and a blessedness about stargazing that I love.

When I was a boy, I preferred the sun. I hated to see that evening sun go down and darkness come. When I got about 17, my fancy turned strangely from the sun to the moon. In a most peculiar way, the sun lost its fancy; I loved the moon. But now in these years of baldness, bifocals, bridges, bulges, and bunions, I have come to enjoy more the sedate quietness of the stars! I'm satisfied many of you would testify the same.

David looked up at the stars one night and quoted those words that were inspired of God: *"When I consider thy heavens, the work of thy fingers, the moon and the stars, which thou hast ordained; What is man, that thou art mindful of him? and the son of man, that thou visitest him?"*

God Sent a Man to Teach Me

Man is somebody. I hope to elevate the dignity of man to those of us who call Christ our Saviour. I will build this message around an experience that happened to me and teach you a lesson that God taught me when I became pastor of the First Baptist Church of Hammond, Indiana.

I am not a big preacher; I make no pretense at being one. I was reared as an extremely poor boy. When I was called to preach, I thought I would never preach to a hundred people at one time. I had no idea I would ever pastor a church of any size at all. I still consider myself a small preacher. In fact, I think all preachers should stay small preachers in their own sight. Our position is big, but we ought to be small.

When I was called to the pastorate of the First Baptist Church of Hammond, the Lord taught me this lesson the first day in my office. I was unpacking my books one day when the secretary said, "Brother Hyles [and I like the title "Brother"], someone to see you."

I thought perhaps the mayor had dropped by for a visit. Maybe the chairman of the local Chamber of Commerce had come. I straightened my collar and my tie and buttoned my coat and said, "Show him in." The door was open a little bit, and I looked out the crack. Our offices each have a main door to the hall, and there are also connecting doors between the offices. I looked out the crack in the door and saw that it was not the mayor nor the Chamber of Commerce chairman. I saw what we would call a bum off the street. I had never seen a man like him.

Our church is located downtown in Hammond, a city of 125,000 people. Many transient people come by, but honestly, this character was one of the filthiest persons I had ever seen. He had on an old dirty, greasy cap, the kind that has a bill and snaps at the front. His hair was long—it came down like mine did when I was a boy and had mine cut by putting a bowl on top and chopping around the edge. His face was dirty, filthy, and unshaven. His collar was yellow with filth; his shirt was dirty and torn; his trousers had patches on the knees; and his shoes were slit over each toe to allow room for a wide foot.

After looking at him, I said to the secretary, "I'm sorry. I'm busy. I cannot see him." I turned back to unpacking my books. My office was a mess, and I had much to do. I had appointments to keep. I had people to meet. I could not see him.

When she looked at me and asked, "Brother Hyles, are you sure you don't want to see him?" I sighed and said, "Send him in. I'll see him."

After talking to him for a while, I gave him a meal ticket and an old suit of clothes. I tried to get him on his way. And I witnessed to him about the Saviour, as I think every preacher of the Gospel ought to do. I told him how he could be saved. I found he had never been converted and was of a Catholic background. I told him about Jesus.

> *I love* to tell the story,
> For those who know it best
> Seem hungering and thirsting
> To hear it like the rest.
>
> And when, in scenes of glory
> I sing the new, new song,
> 'Twill be the old, old story
> That I have loved so long.

After I had told him the story of salvation through Christ, I said, "May I ask that we kneel and pray." We did. As we went to our knees, he made the usual cross and bowed on his knees like a little boy at the altar. He put his hands under his chin and laid his cap beside him. I asked him to pray, and he prayed the sinner's prayer. I feel he was saved, and he had a blessed experience.

But before he prayed, I prayed. While I prayed, God taught me the lesson that He wanted to teach me on the first days as pastor of the First Baptist Church of Hammond. I knelt to pray, and I will be honest—the odor was unbearable, nauseating. As that fellow bowed and closed his eyes, I looked at his old greasy cap; his long, tousled hair; his dirty and unshaven face; his yellow, filthy shirt; his baggy, ragged trousers; at his split shoes, and I thought, "This is the most miserable wretch I have ever seen in my life."

God Created Earth and All Things for Men

All of a sudden, just as if God Himself had written the eighth Psalm on the wall of my study, I saw it there. I began to think about this man. Here was a man made in the image of God. He was a fallen creature, to be sure; a depraved man, to be sure; and a sinner by nature. Yet here was a man who has been the object of God's love from eternity to eternity, from the making of man in Eden until that day when we will sing, "All hail the power of Jesus' name."

I realized here was somebody. I thought as I looked at that dirty, filthy man, that he was the object of God's love. The first thought that hit my mind was this: "What is man, that thou art mindful of him? and the son of man, that thou visitest him?"

The reason God one day spoke and lilies covered the fields was for this man. The reason God one day bade the water above be separated from the water beneath was for this man. The reason God raised the trees like great spires in the sky was for this man. The reason God raised the mountains like great pyramids on the horizon was for this man. The reason God dotted the land with lakes like heavenly teardrops was for this man. The reason God made the birds' melodious choirs to sing through the heaven was for this man. The reason God made the stars for midnight chandeliers was for this man. All of God's creation was for one man!

There is something that happens to a preacher, and it can easily happen to a young man assuming a position in a large city church, as was my case. That something is this: somehow we lose sight of the fact that God has called us to preach to men. We forget that the purpose of our ministry is reaching men. We are not social gospellers. I like what the old Mississippi Negro preacher said: "I'm gonna kick the Devil as long as I've got a foot. I'm gonna bite him as long as I've got teeth. Then I'm gonna gum him till I die."

Our job is not improving society. Getting people saved will improve society more than all the social programs put together. Preaching the Gospel of Christ will save more alcoholics accidentally on the drippings than Alcoholics Anonymous will save on purpose. Preaching the Gospel of Christ will clean up more slums accidentally than Slum Clearance Committees will do on purpose. Preaching the Gospel of Christ will save more homes accidentally than all the psychologists and psychiatrists will do on purpose. Preaching the Gospel of Christ will save more derelicts and restore more harlots and drunkards and prostitutes than all of the Social Betterment Leagues and the social gospel will do on purpose. The need of this hour, my precious friend, is for churches and preachers and Christians to be consumed in the great task of reaching men with the Gospel of Jesus Christ.

Jesus Came to Save Men

I looked at him. I couldn't help but think as I knelt to pray with him, not only was creation for this man, but Jesus came for this man.

Luke 19:10 says, *"For the Son of man is come to seek and to save that which was lost."* The Saviour said in John 20:21, *"…as my Father hath sent me, even so send I you."* In Luke chapter 15, it was one lost coin, one lost boy, and one lost sheep. At midnight it was one Nicodemus; at noonday it was one woman at the well; on the Cross there was one dying thief; up a tree there was one Zacchaeus; there was one Bartimaeus on the road; there was one lady possessed of seven demons. Our Lord preached His greatest sermons to one person. He gave His greatest discourses to one.

When we preachers get to the place where we are nothing more than somewhat of an Old Mother Hubbard, Santa Claus, and Grandma Moses, we have lost our vision of men as the purpose of the ministry of the Gospel of Christ. God give us some prophets who reap men. God give us some Elijahs, Jonathan Edwardses, Charles G. Finneys, Dwight Moodys, and Billy Sundays. God give us some weeping Jeremiahs and courageous Isaiahs who put men in their sights and seek to reach men.

When I go to a new church, I am often asked to do everything except preach the Gospel of Christ. They want me to pray at the dedication of a new swimming pool, pull the trigger for every beetle race in town, and hold the ceremonies for every garbage can improvement campaign. I try to let them know quickly that my job is not a social ministry—but preaching the glorious Gospel of Christ to men. So Jesus came for men.

Ah, my precious friend, keep your sights on men. It's so easy to build denominations and forget the men. It's easy to build churches and forget men. It's so easy to build hospitals and forget patients. It's so easy to build homes and forget the children. It's so easy to build schools and forget pupils. Our job is not reaching society; our job is not saving the world; our job is reaching that next poor sinner for Jesus Christ.

Jesus Lived for Men

As I looked at him, I continued to think: "Not only did God create the world for this old bum, not only did God send His Son Jesus for this one man, but Jesus lived for one man."

Oftentimes people say to me, "I came by to see your work."

When I reply, "My work is at work," they will say, "What do you mean?"

I say, "Do you want to see my work?"

"Well," they say, "I mean your auditorium."

I say, "My auditorium or my work? My work is not building buildings. My work is not building churches. My work is not building Sunday schools. My work is building men for Jesus."

When I was in Texas pastoring, we had 13 mission points or branch churches scattered around the area. One of our young men was Carmen

Hartsfield, an all-conference center of the high school football team and the president of the senior class of his large 2,000-member high school. Carmen was also a preacher boy who pastored one of our mission chapels in a little neighborhood called Spring Creek Community, five miles north of Garland, Texas. One Saturday afternoon Carmen was wearing workclothes when he came to our church to ask me if he could borrow some chairs for the chapel.

"Take them right on, Carmen," I said. "Get yourself a big stack of them and load them on your pickup truck."

One of our fellows whose first name was Cortez was there that day. Cortez, at that time, was a very demonstrative-type person (which means he said "Amen" occasionally during the preaching). Cortez was also in workclothes, so Carmen said to him, "Cortez, would you mind helping me load the truck, take the chairs out to the chapel, and set them up?"

Cortez said, "Well, I guess I will."

They put the chairs in the back of the pickup truck, drove to the little chapel in the country, and proceeded to set up the little auditorium for services the next morning. When they had finished setting up the auditorium, Cortez said, "Carmen, I am feeling backslidden today. I'm cold in my heart. I need to get my old heart warmed."

My 18-year-old preacher boy said, "Well, I happen to have my Bible with me, and in this Bible is my prepared sermon for tomorrow morning. If you will sit on the back row, I will preach to you. I think the message I have prepared will warm your heart."

So, with his overalls on, the Reverend Hartsfield approached the pulpit to preach the sermon to one man. His friend Cortez sat alone in the back row. But my young preacher boy hadn't learned how to preach yet. (I think oftentimes that is a tremendous advantage.) He just stood up and said, "You better get born again or you're going to Hell. Jesus is wonderful. Hell is hot. Sin is black. Salvation is tremendous. It sure is good to be saved."

Back in the back Cortez would say, "Amen! Praise the Lord! That's great preaching!"

Carmen had preached about ten minutes with Cortez shouting

"Amen" from the back when the side door opened. An 18-year-old lad walked in. It was five o'clock on Saturday afternoon. If you were to walk into a little chapel and find one overalled fellow in the pulpit hollering, "You'd better get born again or you're going to Hell," and one fellow sitting alone in the back row, "Amen! Preach on! Let him have it," how would you feel?

The stranger removed his hat and sat down on the front row. Carmen didn't break stride and didn't even stop to welcome the visitor; he just kept on preaching to his audience, which now consisted of two. Forty minutes later when Carmen finished the sermon (he hadn't learned that you can't preach but 20 minutes), he said, "Gentlemen, let's bow our heads for prayer.

Cortez and the visitor bowed their heads. Carmen asked, "Is there anyone here who wants to be saved? Is there anyone here who does not know that he is saved, but wants to be saved?"

That young 18-year-old fellow raised his hand! Carmen said, "Now we're going to stand and sing, 'Just as I am without one plea.' " When the singing started, that 18-year-old boy came down the aisle and was gloriously saved that day!

Don't ever get above reaching people for Christ. Don't ever get to the place where you are a servant for society. Don't ever get to the place where you lose your passion for that next man who needs to be saved by the grace of God.

Jesus Died for Men

So I looked at this bum with his dirty hat, his filthy and unshaven face, his shirt yellow with filth, his patched trousers, and his split shoes with holes in the bottom. A terrible odor emanated from him. The Lord continued teaching me this lesson I am sharing with you. Not only did Jesus create the world for this man; not only did Jesus come for this man; not only did Jesus live for this man; but Jesus died for this man.

Why did Jesus take the spittle of Calvary? To improve society? No! He did it so that one man could be saved. Why the nails in His hands and feet? Why the spear in His side? Why the spittle upon His face? Why the slapping and backhanding and mocking? Why the sign on Him saying, "This is Jesus, the King of the Jews"? Why the mock reed and mock robe? Why the crowd coming by and hurling insults at Him? Why the nudeness and embarrassing moments of Calvary? Why? To improve society? To bring in the kingdom by human efforts? No! All this was so that people fallen away from Christ by sin might come one at a time and find redemption and salvation through the precious blood of our Saviour Who died for one man.

You are somebody! Jesus died for you! You might be a little widow. The mailman may not stop often at your house. The children may not write as they should write. You may not be well-known in your neighborhood. But you are somebody in the sight of God. You may be a poor man; you may be a small child; you may be a timid introvert, but you are somebody in the eyes of God. God made the world for you. He loves you. He came for you. He lived for you. And then, He died for you.

I preached this same message in a conference in Durham, North Carolina. After I had finished preaching, the moderator asked, "Does anyone have a word to say?"

A little, old, shriveled-up, retired preacher, skinny as he could be and looking like a peach after the frost had bit, came to the platform. (God bless him, I love little preachers!) He looked out at that audience of people with his great protruding eyes and said, "Ladies and gentleman, for 50 years I have been looking forward to retiring. Six months ago, I finally retired. I am now receiving my pension. My body is feeble and worn, and I never thought I amounted to much for God. But this morning I realized I am somebody!" He threw back his tired old shoulders and raised his little skinny arms upward and said, "I'm reenlisting to preach some more of the glorious Gospel of Jesus Christ!"

You may be a small preacher with a small salary, but you are somebody to God!

Isn't it wonderful! The importance of the individual is the difference between Russian Communism and American democracy, and Christ's Christianity. It's not the individual for the state, but the state for the individual.

I have a motto for my ministry, and it is printed on the front page of my book, *How to Boost Your Church Attendance*: "I do not want to use my people to build my work, but I want to use my work to build my people." That's our job—building people, reaching people.

So as I looked at my unkempt visitor, the Lord taught me yet another lesson I needed to learn.

The Holy Spirit Comes to Dwell in Men

As I continued thinking, *"What is man, that thou are mindful of him? and the son of man, that thou visitest him?"* I was reminded not only did God create the world for this man, not only did God send His Son for this man, not only did His Son live for this man and die for this man, but the Holy Spirit came in power to indwell believers individually. I like that! The Holy Spirit did not come on Pentecost to indwell a building or live in a sanctuary. He came to indwell the bodies of born-again people.

Dr. George W. Truett gave the following illustration about his five-year-old granddaughter who came to the office one day with him, and I think it is so near to what I am trying to say.

Dr. Truett was trying to study, and those who have children know how it is. As he was trying to concentrate, his little granddaughter said, "Granddaddy, I want a drink of water."

Dr. Truett said, "All right, all right. I will get you a drink of water." After he gave her the drink, he said, "Now honey, I'm trying to study. Would you be quiet and leave me alone?"

"Yes, Granddaddy, I will." And she meant it. Five minutes later though, he heard, "Granddaddy, could I have a drink please?"

After getting her another drink of water and thinking it would pacify her, he said, "Leave me alone; I'm busy."

Finally, a thought hit him. A jigsaw puzzle of a map of the world was on his desk. He thought, "It will take her all day to put this puzzle together. How would she know where to put all the nations of the world?" So he said, "Sweetheart, would you like to put a jigsaw puzzle together?"

"Oh yes, I would, Granddaddy," she replied. "I like to put jigsaw puzzles together."

He put her on the floor in the outer office and scrambled the puzzle pieces; then he said to her, "When you get through, show it to me."

Five minutes later, he heard her voice from the outer office, "Granddaddy, it's all together."

"You mean you put the world together in the last five minutes?"

"Yes, Granddaddy, it's all together."

He thought she was exaggerating, so he walked into the room. To his amazement, there it was—all put together. "Sweetheart, where did you learn this?" he asked. "Did you do it by yourself?"

"Yes, by myself."

"Did you know where to put the countries?"

"I didn't know where to put any countries."

"How did you do it?"

"Granddaddy," she answered, "on the back of the map there was a picture of a man. I just got the man right, and the world took care of itself."

Don't Forget the Individual!

If we will go after man, the world will take care of itself. There's something that happens between the call of God when God anoints him and supernaturally calls him and the time when somehow or other he becomes a bigshot. That's the saddest day in the life of a preacher. For many a preacher, it was a sad day when he got his first blue serge suit and his first private telephone.

I looked at him, and I saw his dirty cap, filthy face, unshaven long beard, yellow shirt, patched trousers, and holey shoes. I thought, "Heaven's joy is over one sinner who repents."

When your church raises a budget, Heaven smiles. When the Sunday school breaks its record, Heaven grins. When the pastor adopts the program for the year, Heaven laughs. But when one little girl or one stumbling, drunken bum comes down the aisle of a church to accept Christ, Heaven becomes a great holy-roller camp meeting, and they rejoice over that one sinner who repents.

I had learned a lesson. I looked at him, and all of a sudden, he was twisting a derby hat in his hand. His hair was neatly combed and freshly cut. His face was clean and freshly shaven. His shirt was white as the snow. His tie matched the socks. The suit was freshly pressed. His shoes were new and neatly shined. His scent was a sweet-smelling perfume.

I got off my knees that day, bowed before him humbly, took his hand, and said, "Sir, I am so glad you came by today. What an honor it has been to have you, a man made in the image of God, visit my office today."

He looked at me as if he had seen a ghost. The last I saw, he was twisting that old dirty cap in his hands as he walked out the door. That was a wonderful lesson to me. I thought again, *"What is man, that thou art mindful of him? and the son of man that thou visitest him?"*

But it doesn't stop there. One Saturday night my little boy David, who was six years old at the time, and I went to a rescue mission to preach. My wife was in the hospital, just having given birth to our fourth child. Right before I was to speak, the superintendent said, "And now my assistant at the mission is going to play the guitar and sing a song."

Many days had passed since that morning in my office when God taught me some lessons about the dignity of man. A very neatly dressed young man walked down the side aisle. I was sitting on the front row. He walked to the platform and gave the testimony of how he had just been converted a few months ago. I said, "David, where have I seen that fellow?"

"I don't know him, Daddy," David answered.

"I have seen him somewhere, David."

He stood up to play his number and sing, and it struck me. That was him! I smiled. He looked at me, and I looked at him. I thought of the Psalm, *"What is man that thou art mindful of him? and the son of man that thou visitest him?"*

My friends, that little primary child who toddles down the aisle in your church on a Sunday morning with ragged clothes and long, shaggy hair is somebody to God. That old drunken bum staggering down Skid Row looking for the next cigarette thrown away by the one before is somebody to God.

If we start to reach people for Christ, we will have to put men in the sights of our spiritual gun and shoot at men. *"What is man that thou art mindful of him? and the son of man that thou visitest him?"*

I saw God wash the world last night
   With His sweet showers on high;
And then when morning came I saw
   Him hang it out to dry.

He washed each tiny blade of grass
   And every trembling tree;
He flung His showers against the hills
   And swept the billowy sea.

The white rose is a cleaner white,
   The red rose is more red
Since God washed every fragrant face
   And put them all to bed.

There's not a bird, there's not a bee
   That wings along the way,
But is a cleaner bird and bee
   Than it was yesterday.

I saw God wash the world last night
   And I would He had washed ME
As clean of all MY dust and dirt,
   As that old white birch tree.
                              -William Stidger

May God wash us and help us to go get men, reach men from house to house, knocking on doors, preaching to men, working for men, witnessing to men, giving our lives for reaching men, whether they be French or Canadian, English or American, whether they speak English,

French, or Spanish. May God helps us always to say with the Psalmist: *"When I consider thy heavens, the work of thy fingers, the moon and the stars, which thou hast ordained; What is man, that thou art mindful of him? and the son of man, that thou visitest him?*

CHAPTER 5

THE SIMPLICITY
OF
SALVATION

Some people, when they use the word "salvation," understand nothing more by it than deliverance from Hell and admittance into Heaven. Now, that is not salvation: those two things are the effects of salvation.

– Charles Spurgeon

The Simplicity of Salvation

"...The word is nigh thee, even in thy mouth, and in thy heart: that is, the word of faith, which we preach." (Romans 10:8)

How easy it is to become a Christian! Occasionally someone will say, "Brother Hyles, you make it so easy to be saved." I always answer, "I did not make it easy; God made it easy. I simply tell you how God made it."

I made this comment in a home recently: if my girl Becky, who is ten, ran away from home, I would want her back. It would be the easiest thing in this world for her to get back. All she would have to do is come and say, "Daddy, I want to come home," and she would be as good as at home. I would want her to come home as much or more than she would want to return, so I would make it very easy for her to come back home.

If one of your children got lost, you would make it easy for him to come back. You would search everywhere. You would be the aggressor. You would be more anxious or at least as anxious for him to come home as he would be to return home.

Our Heavenly Father is the same way. Salvation is not hard; it is simple. Salvation is not running an obstacle course and hoping you will end up standing up someday when the judgment comes. God has made salvation so simple that the smallest child who understands right from wrong can accept it and be saved. God has made salvation so easy that anybody who knows he is a sinner and knows that by faith he can receive Christ as Saviour can be saved.

God's Part in Salvation Is Big, Tremendous

Now, to be sure, salvation is big. We stumble over its bigness in an effort to make it complicated. But bear this thought in mind: all the bigness of salvation is on God's part, not ours. All the immensity and all the working and all the business and all the complexity and all the theology and all the deep doctrine and all the philosophy of being saved is God's part. Our part is so simple.

Salvation is surely big. Man sinned in the Garden of Eden. God made a man; He made a woman. He put them in the Garden of Eden and said, *"...Of every tree of the garden thou mayest freely eat: But of the tree of the knowledge of good and evil, thou shalt not eat of it...."* (Genesis 2:16, 17)

But man ate that forbidden fruit when Satan tempted and tested and deceived Eve. Eve came back and told Adam she had eaten of the fruit, that it was a tree that would make men wise, good to look upon, and it opened her eyes concerning good and evil. Man had sinned. Man was made in the image of God for fellowship with God. When man departed from God, then God made a plan to save man. Now the making of that plan was complex. The making of that plan was eternity-shaking. The making of that plan was big and magnificent, but the receiving of that plan is just as simple as taking a drink of water.

God immediately said, "I am going to make a plan." When Adam and Eve sinned, and sin came into the human race, and man departed from God, immediately God started to make a plan. Jesus Christ, the Son of God, said, "Father, I will go to earth and become man. I am willing to become flesh. I will live a sinless life, a perfect life. I will go to Calvary. I will dip My own soul into Hell itself. I will become sin for man. If man will simply receive Me, he can be saved." Immediately God promised that the seed of woman would bruise the head of the serpent. And the seed of woman would, of course, someday come. Four thousand years later in Bethlehem's manger came the Lord Jesus Christ.

Satan, then, set out to block the coming of the Saviour. He set out to block salvation's plan. Adam and Eve had a boy they named Cain and another boy named Abel. There was the seed of the promised Messiah. But Cain killed Abel, and the seed-carrier was broken. God gave another son whose name was Seth. From the time Seth was born until Jesus Christ came in Bethlehem, Satan did everything he could to block the coming of the Saviour.

When Jesus' coming was finally announced, Satan tried to get Joseph to put Mary away, to stone her so the Messiah would not be born. Finally, when the Messiah came, there was no place for Him to be born, for Satan blocked any hospital, or hotel, or inn from the Saviour. So the Saviour was born in a manger in Bethlehem.

Then immediately Satan tried to block salvation's plan in the leading of Herod to kill all the male children two years old and under. You recall how the angel came to Joseph in a dream and said, "Flee to Egypt." Once again God had blocked Satan's plan to thwart salvation.

Satan was not finished. He took Jesus one day up to a mountain and tempted Him in the wilderness three times, hoping that somehow sin could enter in the life of Jesus Christ. For if Jesus Christ had been a sinner, He would have had to suffer for His own sin and could not suffer for my sin. But Jesus said, "Get thee behind Me, Satan," and He took the sword of the Spirit and three times struck the Word of God into Satan. Jesus did not yield to temptation.

But Satan wasn't through. You recall when Jesus was on the Cross, they came by, looked up at Him, hissed at Him, and said, "If thou be the Son of God, come down from the Cross." Satan well knew if Jesus Christ would come down from Calvary, salvation's plan would be thwarted. But Jesus did not come down.

Satan wasn't finished then. Jesus was put in a borrowed sepulcher. Joseph of Arimathaea and Nicodemus came and got His body and placed it in a borrowed tomb outside the city of Jerusalem. The Bible says that the Roman government put guards around the tomb to guard the Saviour from coming forth. But, thank God, once again, on that Easter Sunday morning Jesus came forth victoriously, and the Gospel is not finished. For Christ, our perfect Lamb, has been sacrificed, has been buried, rose again the third day, and we do have a Gospel.

It is complicated, to be sure. When a person is saved, he is redeemed. His sins are forgiven. His past is forgotten. He is made an heir of God and a joint-heir with Jesus Christ. He is become sanctified in the beloved. As far as God's wrath is concerned, he is justified. He is saved from Hell, and for eternity He will live with God in Heaven to enjoy the bliss of God's prepared city forever and forever.

Complicated, isn't it? Big, isn't it? Immense, isn't it? Immaculate, isn't it? Wonderful, isn't it? Hard to comprehend, isn't it? Yes, it is. But I say once again, that every part of the complicated Gospel is God's part—not man's part. God has prepared a big meal, which is salvation. Jesus Christ was the Bread of Life. He is the Living Water. He is the Meat of the Word. He is the Milk of the Word. Jesus Christ is the great meal. Salvation has been prepared, and now God tells us, "Come, for all things are now ready."

Man Has Tried to Complicate Getting Saved

It is so easy to be saved. Oh, complicated for God—yet so simple for man. I want to show you about the simplicity of being saved. Man has tried to complicate it. God said, "Come." Isn't that all God said to Adam and Eve? "Come." Isn't that all God said in Revelation 22:17? "And the Spirit and the bride say, Come. And let him that heareth say, Come. And let him that is athirst come. And whosoever will, let him take the water of life freely."

A man made a great supper (a picture of salvation) in Luke 14 and sent his servants at suppertime to say, "Come; for all things are now ready." I want to make one thing clear at the start: you cannot do anything to get saved except come to the Lord Jesus Christ.

Oh, how Satan has tried to complicate it. Satan has tried to make more to salvation than that. People have tried to add their own work to salvation. We want some candles in the church. We want some soft music in the background. We want to learn some confessions of faith and take a catechism. We want to do something ourselves to be saved. We want to feel something shoot in our spine and toes. We want to roll down the aisle and shout, "Hallelujah! I hear angels' wings flapping."

A person may get saved by candlelight, but he won't get saved by the candles.

A person may get saved with soft music playing, but the soft music won't have a single thing to do with his getting saved.

A person may get saved in the baptistery. but the baptistery won't have a thing to do with his getting saved.

A person may get saved the moment he joins the church, but the joining of the church won't have a single thing to do with his getting saved.

When a person gets saved, he may shout, but shouting won't have anything to do with his getting saved.

When a person gets saved, he may cry, but crying won't have a single thing to do with his getting saved.

When a person gets saved, he may say, "Whoopee!" but saying "Whoopee" won't have anything to do with his getting saved.

The way to get saved is to come to Jesus and trust Him by faith. It is the simple plan that God has made. Three things tell us of salvation's simplicity:

Bible Examples of Conversions Show Outward Conditions, and Emotions Vary With Different People

"Oh," you say, "the Apostle Paul." We like to take the Apostle Paul's conversion and make a big to-do about that. A light shone round about him, and Paul was thrown to his face on the Damascus road, and was blinded. All of a sudden Paul said, *"Who art thou, Lord?...what wilt thou have me to do?"* (Acts 9:5, 6)

We say, "Then we ought to have a light shine around about us." No, the light shining around Paul didn't save Paul. Paul's falling on his face didn't save him. The blinding of Paul didn't save him. Paul was saved when he received Christ as his Saviour. It is not the circumstances that save; it is the will saying, "I will come to Christ," which makes one a Christian.

Quit waiting for a feeling. You may not hoot and holler when you get saved. I don't know what you will do or what the results of your salvation emotionally will be, but I know this: the resulting feelings have nothing to do with salvation. Salvation is when a person realizes he is a sinner and Christ is the Saviour and by faith he turns to Christ for salvation. That is what being saved is.

Matthew was sitting one day at the seat of customs when Jesus came in the room. Matthew just left all and followed Jesus. No light for Matthew. No falling on his face for Matthew. Now if Matthew had fallen on his face and cried and shouted and said, "O boy! Hallelujah! I'm born again!" and hugged his neighbors and his wife and rejoiced and rolled in the aisle, he would still have been saved, not because he did those things, but because he had put his faith in Christ.

The Bible tells us that one day Zacchaeus was up a tree. Jesus was coming through the city of Jericho on His way to Jerusalem. Zacchaeus wanted to see Him, but there was a great parade coming through, and since Zacchaeus was a little short fellow and could not see Jesus coming, he climbed a tree and looked down. There came Jesus. Jesus said, *"Zacchæus, make haste, and come down; for to day I must abide at thy house."* (Luke 19:5) Jesus went home with Zacchaeus, and over the supper table or dinner table, Zacchaeus trusted Him. Zacchaeus was saved.

The thief on the cross simply said, *"...Lord, remember me when thou comest into thy kingdom."* (Luke 23:42)

Jesus said, *"...To day shalt thou be with me in paradise."* (Luke 23:43) The publican in Luke 18 beat on his breast and said, *"...God be merciful to me a sinner."* (verse 13)

Jesus said, *"...this man went down to his house justified...."* (Luke 18:14)

The eunuch in Acts, chapter 8, said, *"...See, here is water; what doth hinder me to be baptized?"* (verse 36)

Philip said, *"...If thou believest with all thine heart [that Jesus is the Son of God], thou mayest."* (Acts 8:37)

The eunuch believed. He simply trusted Jesus for salvation, and the Bible says in verses 38 and 39 that they got out of the chariot and *"...they went down both into the water, both Philip and the eunuch; and he baptized him...and he went on his way rejoicing."* The eunuch got saved by trusting Christ.

Zacchaeus got saved by trusting Christ. Matthew got saved by trusting Christ. John got saved by trusting Christ. Peter got saved by trusting Christ. There may have been different circumstances, different environments, different stimuli, different emotional responses, and different atmospheres, but salvation is wrapped up in one thing, and that is, "Come, for all things are now ready." Just come to Christ—that's salvation.

New Testament Figures of Speech
Show the Simplicity of Salvation

I want you to notice that not only do Bible examples show the simplicity of salvation, but so also New Testament comparison. All the way through the Bible are figures of speech. The New Testament figures of speech show the simplicity of being saved. Oh, a lot of you would be saved, but you want a light to strike you in the spine. You want a hypodermic needle to hit you. You want to wiggle and roll down the aisle and feel something coming out of your ears and have springs coming out of your head. You want to have something God doesn't say anything about.

When you get saved, you may have springs coming out of your ears, but you are not saved because you have springs coming out of your ears. You may shout when you get saved, but that won't save you. Salvation is by faith in Christ.

Anyone who knows he is a sinner and knows that he is condemned before God to die and knows that Jesus Christ on the Cross suffered for sinners and will simply come to God and say, "Dear Lord, forgive my sins and save my soul today," can be saved.

Now you may shout, but the shouting won't save you. For example, on any given Sunday at First Baptist Church of Hammond, Indiana, we have many different types of conversions in people who come down the aisles. One person may come down the aisle saying, "Oh, I want to be saved," crying the whole time. One Sunday night we almost had to mop the altar when a lady got through.

Here comes another fellow who says, "I want to be saved," smiling really big. Here comes someone else who says, "I want to be saved," with remorse. Here comes another one who says, "I want to be saved," very straightfaced.

Now is it the smile or the tears or the stimuli or the remorse? No, the thing is they all want to be saved. It is not how they act; it is what they do. If by faith one says "yes" to Christ, that settles that.

Let's notice some comparisons.

The New Testament Compares Salvation to Letting Someone in the Door

In Revelation 3:20 Jesus said, *"Behold, I stand at the door, and knock: if any man hear my voice, and open the door, I will come in to him, and will sup with him, and he with me."* I talked to two young people about Christ, and they were both saved. I explained to them that salvation is a matter of Jesus' knocking at the heart and their opening the door and letting Jesus come in. It is very simple to open the door.

If a friend came to see me and rang the bell or knocked on the door, would I come and say, "Whoopee! Come in"? I wouldn't put it that way at all. Very simply, I would say, "Would you come in, please." He comes in.

Jesus said that salvation is like that. He is out of your life. He is not your Saviour. You have lived without Him. You have never trusted Him. Now you simply say, "Dear Jesus, come in." God says that is salvation.

Getting Saved Is Like Taking a Drink of Water

In John 4:14, Jesus said, *"...whosoever drinketh of the water that I shall give him shall never thirst...."* Revelation 22:17, *"And the Spirit and the bride say, Come....And let him that is athirst come. And whosoever will, let him take the water of life freely."* Taking a drink of water is simple.

Some people get so thirsty that when they take a drink of water, they go "Whoo-oo." Some people say, "Ahh-hh-h." Some just swallow it, and that is it. Who gets the most water? How it makes you feel doesn't have a thing to do with it. Jesus said getting saved is like taking a drink of water. Are you thirsty? Do you know you are lost? Do you know you need Christ? He's the One Who is the water. You take a drink, and He comes in. That's what salvation is like, He says.

Getting Saved Is Receiving a Gift

Romans 6:23, *"For the wages of sin is death; but the gift of God is eternal life through Jesus Christ our Lord."* Ephesians 2:8, 9, *"For by grace are ye saved through faith; and that not of yourselves: it is the gift of God: Not of works, lest any man should boast."* I give a person a gift; he takes it. Is it his? Absolutely! What if he doesn't feel good? It is still his. What if he doesn't shout? It is still his. What if he doesn't cry? It is still his. It is very simple to accept a gift. All you do is reach out and take it and believe it is yours.

Now salvation is that way, the Bible says. Jesus is God's "unspeakable gift." Eternal life is God's gift to man. Anybody who will say, "I am willing to receive the gift," can very simply receive the gift from God.

Getting Saved Is Going Through a Door

John 10:9, *"I am the door...."* John 14:6, *"...I am the way, the truth, and the life...."* Is it very complicated to go through a door? When I leave a service at First Baptist Church of Hammond, I nearly always go through the same door. I walk over, turn the doorknob, walk through the door, and go down the stairs. Is that very complicated? I probably won't shout. I doubt if I will cry or holler. I doubt if I'll laugh. But I will go through the door.

Jesus said that on one side is eternal life; on the other side is eternal death. The difference is a door. Everyone who realizes he is unsaved, realizes that Christ will give him eternal life and will say, "Dear Lord, I do accept You and come through the door of Jesus to salvation"—that minute God makes you His child.

Salvation Is Compared With Coming Home

This is very interesting. Here is a boy in Luke 15 who decides to leave his father. He takes all of his goods, goes to a far country, gets in trouble, looks for a job, can't find a job, finds a job feeding the hogs, and finally starts feeding himself the husks off the corn that the swine would not eat. He eats the cornhusks. Finally, he says, "The servants back home have more than this. Why, the servants back home have some good bread and potatoes and meat and beans. Here I am eating the cornshucks. I'll rise and go to my father." He returns to his father, and his father receives him. Salvation is just going home.

Let's say a family is having a reunion. Some children are coming home. One child says, "Oh, it's so good to be home," in tears. Another says, "Boy, it's good to be home!" Still another says, "Brother, it's wonderful to be home," very sincerely. Another says, "Hello, Mother. How have you been?" Who is the nearest home? It doesn't make any difference if one cries, one shouts, one laughs, one feels good, one sighs—they are all home. The Lord never did say that salvation is like a fellow who cries his way home or shouts his way home. It is like coming home.

Maybe you are lost from God. You are away from God. Jesus Christ is salvation. You need only to say, "Lord, I'm coming home."

> *I've* wandered far away from God,
>> Now I'm coming home;
> The paths of sin too long I've trod,
>> Lord, I'm coming home.

Salvation Is Compared to Saying "Yes" to a Proposal

How many of you married ladies remember very distinctly when you said "yes" to a proposal? Remember when he said, "Will you?" Was it very complicated? How many of you cried when your husband asked, "Will you marry me?" How many of you laughed when you said it? How many of you in your heart felt wonderful, but you didn't show a lot of emotion?

Here is a proposal. I am on my knees, and I say, "Beverly, would you make me the happiest man in all of the world? Would you be mine?"

She says, **"Oh, wonderful! Yes!"** She said "yes" to my proposal, but she may just say, "Oh, [sob] yes!" She is just as hooked as she was the other way! Or she may just say, "Um-hum." No matter how she may say it, she still has done the same thing.

Some folks try to get married just like everybody else got married. It isn't how you responded; it is the question. Jesus said, "Will you be married? Will you come to Me? Will you trust Me?" If you say "yes," you are saved. If you say "no," you are lost. The way you respond has nothing to do with your eternal soul. And so He compares it with a proposal.

Jesus Compares It With Accepting an Invitation.

Jesus told the parable of the man who *"…made a great supper and bade many."* Jesus says, *"Come unto me, all ye that labour and are heavy laden, and I will give you rest."* (Matthew 11:28)

I ask a friend, "Will you come over to my house to eat?" If he hasn't eaten for a week, he may say, **"Brother, will I! Sure!"** Let us suppose he is so full he doesn't want to eat a bite today. "Yes, I'll come." Let us suppose we are having broiled T-bone steak: **"Boy, I'll come!"** Or let us suppose he has been wanting to come to our house for a long time and we haven't spoken in a year, and finally he realizes that we're going to speak again. He says, "Oh, I sure will come."

Now let me ask you: will he be any more invited either way he answers? Not a bit. The way he would do it is to accept the invitation.

Now God says, "I have made a great banquet feast. I have prepared salvation. It is a gift. Would you come? Come." Then somebody will say, "You bet I'll come. I'm so far in sin, I'll come"—weeping.

Someone else says, "Yes, I need the Lord. I'll come"—very serious.

Somebody else says, **"A banquet? I'll come!"**—rejoicing.

Somebody else says, "Whoopee!"—smiling.

No matter how you act, you won't get any more to eat. The thing that makes you come is when you say "yes" to the invitation.

Some folks want to get a candle, walk down the aisle with a long flowing robe, and say, "I come." Some want to do cartwheels and flop down the aisle and say, "I come." Some want to cry, "I come." Any way is all right with me, as long as you don't trust that candle, or those cartwheels, or that feeling, or those tears, or that joy to save you. As long as you trust the eternal Word of God and what He said, you have salvation. Would to God that folks could understand it. God simply said, "Come." Man has been trying to make religions, to major on the minors, and major on the sidetracks, and major on the sidelines, when the truth is, all you have to do to be saved is just come to the Lord Jesus Christ.

Again He Compares It With Taking a Bath

Let me illustrate. In Titus 3:5 He says, *"Not by works of righteousness which we have done, but according to his mercy he saved us, by the washing of regeneration."* In John 13 Jesus said, "You have already bathed once; now wash your feet." Salvation is compared to taking a bath. But remember, Jesus is the One Who bathes you, makes you clean.

Many of you take a bath once a week—whether or not you need one! It is not a big chore to take a bath. There have been times when I have been really hot—like on a blistering hot Texas day with the temperature at 109°. I recall it was 111°, and I laid oak floor all day long. I almost died. I got home and said, "Honey, I want a cold bath." We turned on the cool water, and I jumped in. As I jumped in, I said, "Whew-ew!"

There are other times I have had to take a bath really quickly, so I just rush in and rush out. I am just as clean either way. You see, it doesn't matter whether or not you say "Whew-ew." If you want to say "Whew-ew," that's all right. But you don't have to say it to take a bath. Taking a bath is very simple. You know you are dirty; Jesus has the soap. You get in; He bathes you. Now the sidelines may be different. The effect may be different. The outward results may be different. But the bath is the same. You get in and take the bath. Jesus says that salvation is that way. He cleanses all who come for "the washing of regeneration."

Some of you are so dirty and you have been so far into sin that when you jump into salvation, you are going to realize that you are clean, and you will say, "Whoopee! I'm clean!" Some are going to say, "I have been so dirty; it's so good to be clean"—crying all the time. Some are going to say, "I'm so glad to be saved." Some, "Yes, it's good to be a Christian." Now it all depends on how dirty you are. It all depends on how hot it has been. It depends on how much you need the bath. But the salvation is not the *whoopee* or the *whew-ew* or the joy or the thrill or the tears. It is getting in the tub and taking the bath.

Salvation Is Compared to Putting Money in the Bank

II Timothy 1:12, *"I...am persuaded that he is able to keep that which I have committed* [or deposited] *unto him against that day."* You take some money and put it in the bank. Two fellows go to the bank, and each one deposits $100. One says, "**O boy! O boy!** I saved $100." The other quietly says, "Me too." Which one has saved $100? Both have. You mean how happy you get about the money doesn't mean who has the $100 in the bank? That is right. The question is not, did you shout to the teller or cry to to the teller or hit the teller? The question is, did you give the money to the teller?

Many folks say, "I'm saved because I shouted and felt it all over." That is not why a person is saved. A person is saved because he put his soul in the hands of Jesus.

You say, "I was there when it happened, and I ought to know." Pretty song, but it isn't enough. Sure you were there when it happened, and yes, you ought to know. But you are not saved because you were there when it happened. You are saved because you trusted Jesus. You are saved because you said "yes" to Calvary and said, "I will deposit my soul to Jesus' keeping."

Getting Saved Is Like Eating a Meal

The Bible says, "Come, all things are now ready." When we get home from church, some little boy is going to say, "Mom, is dinner ready?"

"Yes, Son."

My little boy David only hits the floor about twice. He dives in. "O boy, Mom! O boy! Got some gravy?"

I walk in, look, say, "Gravy again."

We eat the same gravy. No difference at all—same thing.

Becky might say, "Hot dog!"

David might say, "Whoopee!"

I might say, "I'm so hungry, I've got to get to the food." But we each eat the same food. How we eat it has nothing to do with it. Some fellow can sop it, another can eat it with a spoon. Some fellow can lick it up, another can eat it with a fork. Some fellow can put it on toast, and another can put his biscuits in it. But it is the same gravy. I'm saying, it isn't what happened when you got saved—the experience, etc. It is, did you trust Jesus and did He save you?

Old Testament Types
Show the Simplicity of Getting Saved

Not only do Bible examples and New Testament comparisons show the simplicity of salvation, so also do Old Testament types.

- A coat of skins God offered Adam and Eve. What did they do? They took it; that is all.
- A brazen serpent on the pole in Numbers. Those bitten and dying could only look at that brazen serpent and be saved.
- An ark in Noah's day. What did they have to do? Come inside the ark. That's all—just come inside.
- The little lamb that was slain. What did a Jew have to do? Put his hand on the head of the lamb.

Old Testament types show how simple it is on our part to be saved. To be sure, when you come to Christ, your sins are forgiven. You are made a new creature. The Holy Spirit comes in to live. You become one of God's children. You will go to Heaven. Big! Oh, yes! Immense! But God does all the work. All you do is take it by faith.

Let me illustrate. Recently in visitation I went to the home of a lady who now sits in church. We knelt and prayed, and she said, "Yes, I know I ought to do it. I know I ought to do it."

I said, "Will you do it?"

"Yes," she said, "I will." We knelt to pray. I think with some emotion in her heart but not much in her voice, she said, "Dear Lord, I confess my sins. I pray You will forgive me. I receive You as my Saviour now." She received Christ.

I went down the street a little further. There were two young people who are now attending church. I explained to them. One teenage girl would not look at me but kept looking down. I told her how to be saved, how she would not have to worry any more about going to Hell. Finally she prayed.

Afterward I asked, "Now are you saved?"

"Oh, yes," she said.

And that girl who hesitated to decide and then timidly turned to Jesus in her heart was saved.

The other girl was joyful, immediately happy. But both girls were saved just alike the moment they put their trust in Jesus.

Will You Take Christ and
This Simple Salvation Today?

You have read this sermon showing how simple it is to receive Christ. You can open the door, and Jesus will come in. You can simply receive salvation as a gift. You can accept the sweet invitation. Jesus said, *"...and him that cometh to me I will in no wise cast out."* (John 6:37) If you realize that you are a lost sinner who needs saving and if you are tired of sin and want forgiveness, then I beg you here and now to say "yes" to Jesus in your heart, turn over your case to Him, and depend on Him to do the saving which He promised. Will you do that today?

Pray this simple prayer: *Jesus, I confess that I am a lost sinner who needs forgiveness and salvation. I believe You died on the Cross to save me, so now I trust in You. I accept Your invitation and depend on You to forgive my sins, save my soul, and take me to Heaven when I die. I will set out to live for You, and I will claim You openly as my Saviour.*

If you have decided to trust Christ, please sign the decision form below, make a copy, and mail it to Prepare Now Resources.

Prepare Now Resources
507 State Street
Hammond, Indiana 46320

Signed _____

Address _____

Email Address _____

CHAPTER 6

OTHERS

Sympathy is no substitute for action.

– David Livingstone

Others

(Preached at Bob Jones University; December 3, 1964)

"And about the ninth hour Jesus cried with a loud voice, saying, Eli, Eli, lama sabachthani? that is to say, My God, my God, why hast thou forsaken me?" (Matthew 27:46)

"Then said Jesus, Father, forgive them; for they know not what they do. And they parted his raiment, and cast lots." (Luke 23:34)

"And Jesus said unto him, Verily I say unto thee, To day shalt thou be with me in paradise." (Luke 23:43)

Many years ago, it is said, there was a Salvation Army Convention in a large city—I think it was in London, England. It was during the later years of the famous founder of the Salvation Army, General Booth. General Booth was in ill health, aged, and nearly blind. So the convention was conducted for the first time without the presence of the founder and leader. Someone suggested that General Booth perhaps could send a telegram or a wire to greet the messengers.

Sure enough, when the thousands of delegates were seated, a message came from General Booth. The moderator of the convention opened the telegram and began to read. And here is the message:

"Dear delegates: 'Others.' (Signed) General Booth."

Others
Lord, help me to live from day to day
In such a self-forgetful way,
That even when I kneel to pray
My prayer shall be for others.

Others, Lord, yes, others,
Let this my motto be,
Help me to live for others,
That I may live like Thee.

–Charles D. Meigs

One thing that characterized the life of our Lord as much as any other single thing was that He lived and died for others. His motto was others. His activities were built around others. His desire was to help others. This was found in no other place as vividly as on the Cross of Calvary.

It is interesting to note that in the seven sayings of Christ on the Cross, before Jesus ever used a personal pronoun He used the second and third person. Before He ever said "I" or "Me," He spoke of "them" and "you." He did not say, "I thirst," until He had said, "...*Father, forgive them....*" He did not say, "...*My God, my God, why hast thou forsaken me?*" until He said, "...*Woman, behold thy son,*" and to His disciple, "...*Behold thy mother!*" Even in His death Jesus was thinking not of Himself, but of others. There can be and will be no successful ministry or successful life for Christ until a person has adopted the philosophy that it does not matter a great deal what happens to me, but I will bathe my life and bathe my ministry in the service of others and in the service of the Lord Jesus Christ.

I want to call your attention very briefly to three statements that our Lord made before He spoke of Himself. Each of these first three sayings that He made on the Cross were of others.

- First, Jesus died loving others.
- Secondly, He died caring for the physical needs of others.
- Thirdly, Jesus died saving others.

I. Jesus Died Loving Others

He said, *"...Father, forgive them...."* (Luke 23:34) Before He ever spoke of His own physical needs, before He ever said, *"...into thy hands I commend my spirit..."* (Luke 23:46), before He ever said, *"...My God, my God, why hast thou forsaken me?"* (Matthew 27:46), and before He ever spoke about the first person, He spoke about others. He died loving others.

There are millions of people in this world today to whom no one has ever said, "I love you." In 1861, on the Senate floor, Charles Sumner was nearly killed in a fight. Senator Sumner was asked, after he had recovered, what was the thing that he thought about most while he was on what he thought was his deathbed. Mr. Sumner said, "The thing that I thought about most was I had lived, I was dying, and I had never heard anyone say, 'I love you, Charles.' "

A man sat in my office just a few months ago. He said, "Pastor, I am 26 years old. But until I walked in the doors of the First Baptist Church of Hammond, nobody in 26 years had ever said, 'I love you.' " Oh, there are thousands of people today whom no one loves and who have never heard the blessed words, 'I love you.' "

I have never lived 24 hours without somebody saying, "I love you." Often at night before we go to bed, after we have our Bible study, spend about ten minutes on some character development for our children, and have our prayer time, I say, "Everybody that wants to kiss me, line up here." (The line is usually a little scarce when I stand!) My little girl, Cindy, who is five, is always the first. Then my little girl, Linda, is next and David, who is ten, reluctantly stands in line. Then Becky, who is 13, stands in line. They kiss me, and as each child kisses me, he says, "I love you, Daddy."

And I say, "I love you, Cindy."

Then the next one says, "I love you, Daddy."

And I say, "I love you, Linda."

"I love you, Daddy."

"I love you, David."

"I love you, Daddy."

"I love you, Becky."

Then Mrs. Hyles says, "Good night, honey!"

Then little Cindy will stand up and say, "Anybody that wants to kiss me, line up here." (It takes us fifteen minutes for our devotions and two hours to kiss good night!)

But many, many times a day I have the blessed privilege of hearing those words—"I love you."

I am saying this: I believe in an exchange of tender affection, and I believe in expressing love. Yet people walk the streets of your town and mine for whom no one cares. Churches don't care. Preachers don't care. If we are going to be successful, we must have the spirit of Jesus Christ, and we must live and we must die loving others.

Our church in Hammond operates 17 bus routes. Weekly, over 500 people come to Sunday school and church on buses. Our buses cover the entire Calumet area. On Sunday morning men and women, boys and girls come on these buses. Many of them are not well-to-do people; many of them are poor. Their little coats are hand-me-downs. The boys have hair so long you don't know whether to call them she or he. They come because we love them. They know there is one church in town that loves them. They know there is one church in town that is glad to have them. They know there is one church in town that welcomes the poor just like she welcomes the rich. They know there is one church in town that is happy to welcome little boys and girls, men and women for whom no-body cares and whom nobody loves.

They often line up outside the baptistery door to get my autograph. (We baptize every Sunday morning and every Sunday night.) I will kiss the little ones and give them autographs. (The other day a boy asked me for my autograph. I checked, and it was the fifty-third time I had written my name in his Bible!)

One little girl came not long ago, and she asked, "Would you sign my Bible?"

I said, "Yes." She was about six or seven, wore tennis shoes, and her hair was straight. Nobody curled her hair on Saturday night. Nobody polished her shoes. Nobody would greet her at home when she returned and say, "Honey, did you learn anything in Sunday school?" Her father was a drunkard; her mother was a prostitute. But this little girl heard me say one time that I loved her.

I said, "I love you, honey." And every time she would pass me, she would say to her friend, "He loves me. He said he did." She called me, "Mr. Brother Hyles."

She would say, "Mr. Brother Hyles, you are my best friend. You are my best friend." She would pronounce it "fran." "You are my best fran." Every Sunday she would come.

So this little girl said, "You are my best friend." One morning she came and said, "Mr. Brother Hyles, you are my best friend, and I am moving out of town."

I said, "Honey, I am sorry you are moving."

She said, "I said, you are my best friend, and I won't be coming here anymore."

I said, "Honey, I am going to miss you."

She said, "Did you hear what I said? You're not going to get to see me anymore. And you're my best friend!"

I said, "Well, honey, I am so sorry, and I wish I could see you, and I hate to see you move."

The little girl, poor little thing, put her hands on her hips and looked up at me and she said, "Well, ain't you gonna cry?"

And I said, "Yes, I am," and I did. We wept together, and I kissed her goodbye. No one to love her; no one cares for her.

Oh, listen, my young friend, did you ever get the taste one time of the heavenly manna of living for others and saying with the writer:

> Others, Lord, yes others,
> Let this my motto be,
> Help me to live for others
> That I may live like Thee.

One taste of that and you never will be satisfied any more as long as you live with the taste of selfishness, covetousness, and the self-life.

II. Jesus Died Caring
for the Physical Needs of Others

Before He ever said, *"I thirst,"* He said, *"...Woman, behold thy son!"* (John 19:26) Before He ever said, *"...My God, my God, why hast thou forsaken me?"* He said, *"...Behold thy mother!"* (John 19:27) He died caring for their physical needs. He said to the beloved one, "Take care of My mother." He said to His mother, "Here is one to take care of you." Even at His death on the Cross, Jesus died caring for the physical needs of others.

With all of my heart I believe that the church of Jesus Christ and the people of God ought to spend 52 weeks a year supplying the physical needs of people who are destitute and in need. In our church in Hammond, we don't give out Thanksgiving baskets, and we don't give out Christmas baskets—we give out 365-days-a-year baskets for those who are in need. We have a room, almost as big as this platform, full constantly of food and clothing. We have a rescue mission that is operated 365 days a year. It is owned, operated, and sponsored by our church. We feed three meals a day, every day of the year, and have two services a day. We give out food baskets constantly, for we believe that the Gospel of Jesus Christ does have some social applications, and these are in the helping and the caring for the needs of others.

Not only that, but did you know that when you start living the "others life," you will be happier yourself? The Master said it when He said, *"He that findeth his life shall lose it: and he that loseth his life for my sake shall find it."* (Matthew 10:39)

One of our dear members, a sweet lady who is very cultured and refined, came to me about a year ago and said, "Pastor, I am about to have a nervous breakdown."

I said, "I'm sorry."

She said, "Can you help me?"

I said, "Lady, here is what you do. If you will do something for others every day, you won't have a nervous breakdown. Tomorrow take a dozen roses and go to the hospital. Find the rooms where no one is visiting during visiting hours. Walk in and give a rose to each person who is lonely.

The next day go down to the home for the blind, take some candy, and pass it out to the dear blind people. Visit with them a while. Then the next day bake a cake for one of the dear deaf members of our church. If you will do something every day of your life for somebody else, you will not have a nervous breakdown."

She went out to do so. A few months later she said, "Pastor, I have called off the nervous breakdown."

She had found the answer. In the service of others, she had found the happiest life in the world.

It is said that the invalid Elizabeth Barrett Browning was made well because someone loved her and cared for her. When Robert Browning came to Elizabeth Barrett Browning's bedside, she was bedfast. She could not even sit up. It is said that on his first visit, she lifted her head. On his second visit, she sat up in bed. On the third visit, she eloped with him.

Don't you see what I mean? Thousands of people can be reached if somebody cares.

A successful pastor is one who lives his life for others. The successful church is one who lives for others. The happy life is the life that is built around service for others. Jesus died caring for others.

I recall when I was a kid preacher (I started preaching when I was 19), I surrendered not to be a little preacher, but a big one. I surrendered to pastor the First Baptist Church in Dallas. (That was the largest church in the world at that time, and that, I knew, was the one that I ought to have.) Dr. Tom Malone says, "A preacher is like a wasp. He is bigger right after he is hatched than any other time in his life."

So I said, "Lord, here I am, and I surrendered to become pastor of a large church."

But do you know where I started out? The Marris Chapel Baptist Church in Bogota, Texas, Red River County—19 members and a salary of $7.50 a week. Not a single man owned a suit of clothes or a tie. There was only one car in the church family and only one telephone.

I got down in East Texas, and I looked up to God many a day and said, "Lord, remember me? I'm the incumbent, the pastor that You called to pastor First Baptist Church, Dallas." Well, it seemed the Lord didn't even listen to me. Day after day I said, "Lord, this is not what I had in mind."

One day, ah glad day, I looked out at my little congregation of 19 people. There was Charlie Smith and Wood Armstrong and others, and I said to myself, "These are precious people. How sweet and how precious are these people." I went out between two rows in a cotton patch on Sunday afternoon, and I looked up to God and I said, "Dear Lord, I never realized how wonderful my people are. Would it be all right with You, dear Lord, if I spent my life here at the Marris Chapel Baptist Church?"

The dear Lord put His arms around me and He seemed to say, "My child, this is the place I have been trying to get you in now for a long time. I have something bigger for you now." In a few days He moved me on. Dear friend, until we know what it is to live and die for others, we will never know what it is to have happiness and success for ourselves.

> *Lord*, help me to live from day to day
> In such a self-forgetful way,
> That even when I kneel to pray
> My prayer shall be for others.
>
> Others, Lord, yes others,
> Let this my motto be,
> Help me to live for others
> That I might live like Thee.

III. Jesus Died Saving Others

Jesus died not only loving others and caring for the physical needs of others, but Jesus died saving others. Even in His death, His life meant the salvation of others. There was one Zacchaeus up a tree, one Bartimaeus beside the Jericho Road, one lady at noonday, one Nicodemus at midnight—witnessing, winning souls to Himself, performing miracles. But even at His death, Jesus died saving others. Let me say this: No one can have the kind of ministry that God wants him to have unless he spends his life reaching others with the Gospel of Jesus Christ. Jesus died saving others.

The other day I was in the hospital making a visit. One of our good men was very ill. I walked past the other bed in the room to get to his which was near the window. I did not stop and talk to the man in the first bed. Normally I do, but I was in a hurry to go to our daily morning broadcast. I walked in and had a prayer with my man, and when I started to leave, I heard a voice, the voice of an old man. It was a voice that was quivering. The old man said, "Reverend, Reverend?"

I turned and I saw him, tears rolling down his cheeks. He must have been eighty. He said, "Reverend, would you pray that prayer for me, too? Would you pray that prayer for me, too?" I held his old hand and prayed for him. As I turned to walk out of the room, the old man looked at me with his lips quivering and said, "Reverend, nobody ever prayed for me before. Nobody ever prayed for me before."

Friends, this is a sick world. It is a world of heartache and heartbreak and broken dreams and broken lives and broken aspirations. It is a world that is in need, it is a world that is hungry, it is a world that is miserable, it is a world that is neurotic, it is a world that is brokenhearted. It is a weeping world, it is a needy world—and we have to face it. The only hope we have to be successful in our work is to live our lives in the service of others.

When I went to the city of Hammond nearly five and a half years ago, I did not want to leave my church that I had seen grow from forty-four members to 4,128 members in six and a half years. They were my people. I did not want to leave. The Lord said, "I want you to go to Hammond." I said, "No, no. I don't want to go."

The Choice

I said, "Let me walk in the fields";
 He said, "Nay, walk in the town";
I said, "There are no flowers there";
 He said, "No flowers, but a crown."

I said, "But the sky is black,
 There is nothing but noise and din."

But He wept as He led me back;
    "There is more," He said, "there is sin."

I said, "But the air is thick,
    And fogs are veiling the sun."
He answered, "Yet hearts are sick,
    And souls in the dark undone."

I said, "I shall miss the light,
    And friends will miss me, they say. "
He answered me, "Choose tonight
    If I am to miss you, or they."

I pleaded for time to be given;
    He said, "Is it hard to decide?
It will not seem hard in Heaven
    To have followed the steps of your Guide."

I cast one look at the field,
    Then set my face to the town;
He said, "My child, do you yield?
    Will you leave the flowers for the crown?"

Then into His hand went mine,
    And into my heart came He,
And I walk in a light divine
    The path I had feared to see!
                  –George McDonald

Whether it is in Hammond, Indiana; in the apartment buildings of Chicago; in the plains of Texas; in the deep South; in the mountains of Colorado; in the hills of the East; or on the beaches of the Coast—wherever it is, there is joy, there is peace, there is victory in a life that is lived and, yea, that is given loving others, serving others, and saving others.

CHAPTER 7

THE SOWING, GROWING, AND KNOWING THE TARES

He that lives in sin and looks for happiness hereafter is like him that soweth cockle and thinks to fill his barn with wheat or barley.

– John Bunyan

The Sowing, Growing and Knowing the Tares

"…Gather ye together first the tares, and bind them in bundles to burn them: but gather the wheat into my barn." (Matthew 13:30)

L et us read, in the thirteenth chapter of Matthew, the parable of the tares as given by the Lord Jesus: *"Another parable put he forth unto them, saying, The kingdom of heaven is likened unto a man which sowed good seed in his field: *25*But while men slept, his enemy came and sowed tares among the wheat, and went his way. *26*But when the blade was sprung up, and brought forth fruit, then appeared the tares also. *27*So the servants of the householder came and said unto him, Sir, didst not thou sow good seed in thy field? from whence then hath it tares? *28*He said unto them, An enemy hath done this. The servants said unto him, Wilt thou then that we go and gather them up? *29*But he said, Nay: lest while ye gather up the tares, ye root up also the wheat with them. *30*Let both grow together until the harvest: and in the time of harvest I will say to the reapers, Gather ye together first the tares, and bind them in bundles to burn them: but gather the wheat into my barn."* (Mathew 13:24–30)

Now, for an interpretation of that parable turn to verse 36 of this chapter, and you will find the parable explained…

*"Then Jesus sent the multitude away, and went into the house: and his disciples came unto him, saying, Declare unto us the parable of the tares of the field. *37*He answered and said unto them, He that soweth the good seed is the Son of man; *38*The field is the world; the good seed are the children of the kingdom; but the tares are the children of the wicked one;*

[39]*The enemy that sowed them is the devil; the harvest is the end of the world* [end of the age]; *and the reapers are the angels.* [40]*As therefore the tares are gathered and burned in the fire; so shall it be in the end of this world.* [41]*The Son of man shall send forth his angels, and they shall gather out of his kingdom all things that offend, and them which do iniquity;* [42]*And shall cast them into a furnace of fire: there shall be wailing and gnashing of teeth.* [43]*Then shall the righteous shine forth as the sun in the kingdom of their Father. Who hath ears to hear, let him hear."* (Matthew 13:36–43)

I have been thinking much lately about the parable of the tares, so I started reading it to find out who the tares really represent. I have come to this conclusion: I have been wrong to an extent. I had always thought the tares represent all of the drunkards, harlots, gamblers, etc., who belong to churches. But I have come to this conclusion: if I were the Devil, I would not want that kind of church members. I would want the best. So, I believe that many of the lost church members appear to be the best church members we have.

I used to long for a big church. I used to say if I could ever have a church with a thousand members, I would be the happiest man in the world. Then, when I got a thousand, I wanted two thousand. Now that I have two thousand, I want three thousand. But I have a new goal: I would love to pastor a church some day that is completely regenerated. Wouldn't it be wonderful to have a church in which every member is born again?

Many of you have, some time, somewhere, belonged to a church as an unregenerate church member. Sometimes I wonder if we who preach on this often, who preach and teach that you must be born again, who magnify the plan of salvation—if we have people who are tares. Think about the churches who never hear any preaching about it—how many of them must be unsaved?

I only want people in my church who have been born again. I would not spend 15 minutes of my time going up and down the city begging folks to join my church who have not personally trusted Christ for salvation. What we most need today to solve our problems is a re-emphasis on the new birth. We don't need primarily more training, or more study courses, more seals, more diplomas; rather, we badly need to get some folks saved in our churches.

Now, in the beginning of this message I want to make this statement: **the greatest fifth column in the world is in the church.** If I were the Devil, I would get my members in the best churches in the land, and I would make my members appear the best members in the land. A drunkard in the gutter is not good advertisement for the Devil. An advertisement for the Devil is a good-looking lady sipping cocktails or drinking eggnog at the Christmas party, not a lady with sunken eyes, a wrinkled face, and discolored hair. A man who goes to church on Sunday and goes out to the job as "a man of distinction" is good advertisement for the Devil.

The Sowing

Look at the sowing in verses 24 and 25 of Matthew 13. You recall that the good man spoken of in verse 38 is the Son of man. He is the one who sows seed in the fields. Now, WE are the seed, and the field is the world. It says that "while men slept" the enemy came. The enemy is the Devil.

While men slept, the Devil came and sowed his own seed among the wheat. A tare looks like the wheat—a tare can be mistaken for the wheat. In many churches there is no mistake—they are all of the Devil. But the Devil comes among God's people, among born-again people, and sows seed among them that grows up **with the wheat.** The tare grows side by side with the wheat. You cannot tell them from the wheat. No one but God and the angels can tell them from the wheat. Satan's greatest work is not the drunkard, not the prostitute, not the prison system; but his greatest work is the tare!

One morning I started outside to feed my dog. I put on my hat to cover up my hair and put on my overcoat to cover my pajamas. My little boy David said, "Bye-bye, Daddy." He thought I was going to church because I had put on my hat and coat. I was a tare. On the outside I looked like a fellow going to church. I looked exactly like I looked 30 minutes later when I was ready to get into the car. David thought I was going to church, but when I took off my overcoat and hat, it was a different sight.

A tare cannot be recognized by those who look only on the outside. A tare can only be determined by those who look on the inside. The only ones who can look on the inside of your heart today are you and God and, the Bible says, the angels. **A tare is the greatest work of the Devil.**

When did the tares get sown in the fields? Verse 25 says, *"... While men slept...."* Why do you think we preachers go around all the time trying to wake up people? We are trying to keep the Devil from sowing tares in the church. A fellow said to me recently, "Brother Jack, you holler too loud. You need to be a little softer."

I said, "Now, you listen, friend; your church here has, by a standing vote, only three people who have won anyone to Jesus in the last twelve months. I always make my hollering to a man who is asleep in direct proportion as to how long he has been sleeping and how sleepy he is."

When I was in the service, let us suppose the sergeant came through at six o'clock each morning, and he came to my bunk with a little engraved invitation which said: *"The First Sergeant desires your presence at the Mess Hall at seven o'clock for the observance of the morning meal."*

Then let us suppose he said, "Jackie Boy, if it is all right with you (I don't want to disturb you because you've been giving some money to the company pot lately and you are one of the most influential people in this outfit)—if you are so disposed, and if you don't mind, and if you are not too cold, and if it will not hurt your feelings, would you mind opening brown eyes and trickling on down to the Mess Hall for breakfast?"

And let us suppose I said, "Sergeant, my Aunt Lucy is coming today, and I haven't seen her in six or eight years."

Do you suppose he says, "That's all right—just come when you can"?

Oh, no! He came in and shouted, "You lazy bunch of buzzards, get up! It's five minutes after six—get on your feet! Get up!!! And he used some more words that I cannot repeat. I felt impressed to get up, and I got up.

The average preacher should do the same. We should wake them up!

The tares are sown in the church while we are asleep. If we will stay awake in the church, the Devil will not sow as many tares.

While we are asleep, the tares are coming in. If we don't wake our churches up, we are going to be full of tares. I can tell many churches are run by tares and are full of tares. It happens while we are asleep.

The Growing

Verses 26–28: *"But when the blade was sprung up, and brought forth fruit, then appeared the tares also. So the servants of the householder came and said unto him, Sir, didst not thou sow good seed in thy field? from whence then hath it tares? He said unto them, An enemy hath done this."*

Do you know what we should say? "Now, let's be ethical. They mean well; they are just not dispositioned like we are. Let's not be critical." But the householder declared, "An **enemy** has done this thing."

"...The servants said unto him, Wilt thou then that we go and gather them up?" (Mathew 13:28)

The Lord is preaching to me here; I would like to go gather them up. The passage continues in verse 29, *"...Nay; lest while ye gather up the tares, ye root up also the wheat with them."* We are not to put lost sinners to death. Wait till the harvest! We cannot send them to Hell. Wait till God sends His angels to do that.

"Let both grow together until the harvest...." (Matthew 12:30) Dear friend, it would do you well to examine your own conversion experience. The Bible says, *"Let both grow together...."* Anybody can tell a weed from wheat, but it takes a pretty insightful person to tell a tare. If you are a weed, you know it. If you are a tare, the Devil will tell you that you are wheat.

- **They grow together.** They go to Sunday school together; they go to Training Union together; they do church work together. The Devil puts tares in good churches. He often makes them pray in public; He sometimes makes Sunday school teachers of them. This may sound a little peculiar, but I am persuaded to believe that this chapter teaches that the tares look just about like the wheat. They grow together. They go to church together, apparently may be some of the best members we have, yet the Bible says that they are tares. The Lord said to just let them grow together.

- **Only the angels know them.** Many times a tare looks as much like a Christian as a Christian does. Often the Devil makes his tares look so much like wheat that often they make better looking wheat than the wheat. But they just don't make very good bread. Only the angels know.

The Knowing

We have seen the sowing, the growing; then there comes the knowing. The Lord is speaking in Matthew 13:30, which says, *"Let both grow together until the harvest...."* and it says in the explanation in verses 36 to 43 that the harvest is the end of the age.

Dear friend, the **knowing** is this: the end is coming! Look out, tares, when the end comes! You can fool those who plant, you can fool those who water, you can fool all of those who chop the weeds—they will never chop you. You can fool all of those who irrigate, and all of those who fertilize, but you will **never** fool those who reap.

You looked like wheat, you acted like wheat, you prayed like wheat, but you are a tare. Dear friend, the end is going to come! But you say, "I don't feel bad about this thing." You won't, friend, until the end comes. I don't think that you will feel very bad because as long as you are looking like wheat, as long as folks think you are wheat, there is no reason to feel bad. You know when you'll feel bad? When you are afraid that you are not looking to people like wheat. If the Bible is true, then there will be tares sown among the wheat, and when the harvest time comes, the end of the age, the tares will be found out!

The second thing about the knowing is that the showdown is coming. The angels know.

The third thing about the knowing is in verse 30: *"...Gather ye together first the tares, and bind them in bundles to burn them...."* The tares won't be any good at the harvest because they are no good to anyone. All the tares are going to end in—being burned.

I don't care how good you lived in the harvest field, if you are a tare, you are going to be burned.

- **He knows His own.** May I ask you a question? Are YOU wheat, or are you a tare? How do I know that I am wheat? Dear friend, the Bible says in Romans 10:13, *"For whosoever shall call upon the name of the Lord shall be saved."* Salvation is not crying; salvation is not a sorrow for sin; salvation is not a sorrow for getting caught; salvation is not a turning from sin alone; salvation is receiving Christ by faith completely, realizing that we are sinners condemned by our sin, realizing that Jesus on the Cross died for sinners and that if we will receive Him as our substitute, we can be saved. This is a transaction between the sinner and the Saviour. Examine your heart, as I have examined mine, and **be sure you are wheat.**

CHAPTER 8

YOU CANNOT HIDE FROM GOD

People who are crucified with Christ have three distinct marks: (1) they are facing only one direction, (2) they can never turn back, and (3) they no longer have plans of their own.

– A. W. Tozer

You Cannot Hide From God

(Preached at First Baptist Church, Hammond, Indiana May 3, 1964 • Mechanically Recorded)

PRAYER: "Our Father, fill us, quieten us, speak to us, as we speak on the precious hiding place and that man cannot hide from God but man can hide in God. 'Rock of Ages, cleft for me, Let me hide myself in Thee.' 'I've anchored my soul in the haven of rest, I'll sail the wide seas no more; The tempest may sweep o'er the wild, stormy deep, in Jesus I'm safe evermore.' May we this morning realize we cannot hide from Thee. Quieten the children; cause the young people to behave. May the adults listen intently and carefully as we speak the words from God this morning. Amen."

When our little girl Cindy was smaller, we would play hide and seek. I would hide from her in the closet or in the bathroom or in the bathtub, or go outside the door, or hide behind the door, and I would say, "Come and find me." She would come and look and look and look. Then I would say, "All right, you go hide." She would hide.

She then would say, "Come and find me." And she would be hidden behind the door. I would know where she was, but I would still go look, and I would say, "I wonder where Cindy is?"

She would say, "Right over here."

The next time she would not bother about all the running around and worrying about the trips she would have to take from one room to the other trying to hide. She would just put her hands over her eyes and say, "Come find me." (Anybody who has ever had a child has done this.)

I would say, "I wonder where Cindy is?"

Then she would say, "Right here."

But then when she got older and a little more dignified and a little wiser, she would hold her hands completely over her eyes and say, "Come find me."

I would say, "I wonder where Cindy is?" She would grin out from under her hands. "I wonder where Cindy is?" She was wiser then—she would not tell me. I would look and look and look, and she would think she was hidden. Finally I would say, "There she is. I found you." It disturbed her tremendously because she did not know how I could know where she was. She was completely in the dark. There was nothing to be seen and she would say, "Who told you where I was?" Why, she was there all the time. But she had her own eyes shut, and because she did, she thought I could not find her.

Man is the same way. We have the sneaking idea that we can hide somewhere and drink a glass of liquor and nobody knows about it. We have the foolish, ridiculous idea that man can hide himself from all other men, or a couple can hide themselves on a dark road some night and do things unlawful to God and men—or beasts, for that matter—and God does not see it. But nothing is ever hidden from God. Not an activity, not a book you read, not a word you say, not a thought you think, not a place you go, morning, noon or midnight, is ever hidden from God Almighty. God knows where you are. You are never hidden from Him.

Jeremiah 23:24 says, *"Can any hide himself in secret places that I shall not see him?..."* Jeremiah 49:10 says, *"...he shall not be able to hide himself...."* We read in Ezekiel 28:3, *"...there is no secret that they can hide from thee."* Revelation 6:15 and 16 speak about the end time, and it says that in that time *"...the chief captains, and the mighty men..."* and all the unsaved shall say *"...to the mountains and rocks, Fall on us, and hide us from the face of him* [the living God] *that sitteth on the throne...."* Yet in spite of all of our efforts to have our sins hidden, in spite of all our efforts to hide from God, man never does anything in secret, for the all-seeing eye and the all-hearing ear, the all-searching searchlight of God's eternal omnipotence, shines from Heaven constantly upon our lives, and we never do anything in secret.

Not a kind deed is ever done but what the Heavenly Father will take notice. Not a broken home, not a broken heart, not a broken life, not a cup of water given in His name is ever done or committed but what Jesus does not notice it. And just as really, not a sin is ever committed but that Jesus in Heaven does not see it. You cannot hide from God—neither now nor in the future. Today or in that great day of His wrath, you cannot hide from God. There are three things that man tries to hide from God that he cannot hide from God:

- Man tries to hide his sin.
- Man tries to hide his soul.
- Man tries to hide himself.

Sin Cannot Be Hidden

First, you cannot hide your sin from God. You may think you have a secret sin, but you do not. You may think that because the pastor doesn't know about it, God does not know. You may think it is secret because your mother does not know about it. You may think it is secret because your pastor did not know about it. You may think it is secret because your children do not know about it. You may think it is secret because your father did not know about it.

But my precious friend, were it possible for us to hide our sin one from the other: the pastor would not know, the deacon would not know, the parent would not know—were it possible, it is still impossible to commit any sin that is not under the searchlight of God Almighty.

Isaiah 3:9 says they hide not their sin. Psalm 69:5 says, *"O God, thou knowest my foolishness; and my sins are not hid from thee."* David ought to know; he wrote the Psalms. David, who one day committed that sin with Bathsheba and tried to cover it up; David, who one day found Bathsheba expecting a baby out of wedlock by his own unholy relationship, tried to cover up his sin and hide sin, but finally David in Psalm 69 said, *"...thou knowest my foolishness."*

God knows your foolishness this morning. God knows what you drink; God knows where you go; God knows how you dress; He knows what you say, knows what you hear. There is not a sin committed that is secret, not a one that can be hidden from God Almighty. Jeremiah 16:17 says, *"They are not hid from my face, neither is their iniquity hid from mine eyes."* Hosea 5:3 says, *"...Israel is not hid from me...."* I Corinthians 4:5 says in that day He will bring to light the hidden things of the heart. Psalm 139:12 tells us that *"the darkness hideth not from thee,"* and it goes on to say that day and night is the same with God.

Oh, you may hide your foolishness and your sin in the nighttime from others; you may hide in the nighttime a secret sin from people, but God always sees what you do. The children's song says:

Oh, be careful little hands what you do,
Oh, be careful little hands what you do,
For the Father up above is looking down in love;
Oh, be careful little hands what you do.

Oh, be careful little eyes what you see,
Oh, be careful little eyes what you see,
For the Father up above is looking down in love;
Oh, be careful little eyes what you see.

Oh, be careful little ears what you hear,
Oh, be careful little ears what you hear,
For the Father up above is looking down in love;
Oh, be careful little ears what you hear.

Oh, be careful little feet where you go,
Oh, be careful little feet where you go,
For the Father up above is looking down in love;
Oh, be careful little feet where you go.

May God give us the consciousness of a little child that everything we see, everything we hear, every word we say, every place we go, everything our hands do, is constantly seen by the God Who made us, Who loved us, Who gave Himself for us, Who is coming back for us, Who someday will judge even the hidden secrets of our hearts. God knows your sin.

My young friend, God knows about your sin. Working man, God

knows what you do on the job. You ladies who work in public, God knows what you do. God is constantly looking down and seeing what we do, and He keeps a record constantly of even the innermost secrets of our hearts. Sin will be found out. Numbers 32:23 says, *"...and be sure your sin will find you out."* It may come out a different way.

In Genesis 4:10 God said to Cain, *"...the voice of thy brother's blood crieth unto me from the ground."* The blood of Abel spoke about the sins of Cain. Jesus said one time, "If I do not speak, even these rocks would speak. These stones would cry out."

There is something rather horrifying to me. They are working on an invention where, if it is completed, we can actually hear the words of people who lived thousands of years ago. They say that our voices are recorded even in the rocks, the lumber of our houses. They say that if this world lasts another hundred years, we will probably be able to hear the recorded words of Jesus from the rocks of Jerusalem. Ah, science thinks it is so wonderful. Science says we have discovered and are discovering a way to play back what the rocks said. Jesus said that two thousand years ago! He said the stones would cry out.

Mark it down, my friend, you had better live every day of your life as if your mother watched everything you did. You had better live as if your pastor were watching. Young people at school, you had better do exactly what you would do as if your mother and your father and your pastor were watching everything you did. For not your mother nor your father nor your pastor will judge you, but one day you will stand face to face with Him Who made you, the all-powerful One, and all the hidden deeds of your life, all the words of the mouth, what you hear and say and do and where you go will be brought to judgment.

You cannot hide your sin from God. If nothing else, it will show in your face. I can tell when you have been in sin. I can scan my eyes across this building Sunday after Sunday, and I can tell how you are living. It shows in your face. Sin shows in your face.

Two girls can walk down the street in downtown Hammond. Both of them beautiful; one just as attractive as the other. One can walk 25 feet behind the other. While one girl walks by, she gets the glance and look of lustful men; she hears the cat calls and the wolf whistles of ungodly men. The other girl can walk by—just as beautiful, just as attractive, but she does not get the whistle. Why? Sin shows in your face.

You can tell a gambler nine times out of ten. It is on his face. You can look at a liquor drinker and tell nine times out of ten. It is on his face. It shows on your face what you are.

Even if you could wipe that look of guilt off your face and that look of cynicism off your face while you are in sin, and if you could keep it from being revealed on your countenance, it would bring itself out in your conscience.

Oh, the hounding of the conscience! Oh, if no one else knows it, I know it. I know what I have done. I know where I have been. I know what I have said. I know what I have heard. Oh, the hounding of the conscience!

But if you could hide it from your conscience and if your conscience were seared over with a hot iron as it were, it would still come out some day, because God knows what you do. God sees that parked car. God sees the ice box. God sees your magazine rack. God hears the records you play. God knows what you do on the job. God knows what you do alone. God knows what you do on vacation. Oh, listen, it would change our lives if we could just grasp the fact that every moment of every day and night God Almighty watches what we do and sees what we do.

You say, "It wouldn't affect me, Pastor." Why do you church members burn your fingers trying to put out that cigarette when I come up? I think you should. I don't mean burn yourself; you should put it out and keep it out! Why is it that some of you young people, when you see Brother Hyles, slump down in cars?

I was driving down the street not long ago at night coming back from church and saw one of our young girls so close to the young fellow, they could have had several more in the front seat. Brother, it would have taken them a long time to get unloose from that clench. Let me say this: it is not right, neither is it holy, for a young girl to set her body in such positions as that until she is married and has a license to do it. When she looked around and saw my car (on the front of my car it says First Baptist

Church of Hammond, and they know my car), down she went in an effort to hide! Why? She was afraid for the preacher to see her.

Let me tell you, my young friends, before that preacher ever drove down that street, God in Heaven was watching what you were doing. You cannot hide your sin from God.

You Cannot Hide Your Soul From God

Man can do nothing to hide his soul from God. I call your attention to three verses:

"And they heard the voice of the LORD God walking in the garden in the cool of the day: and Adam and his wife hid themselves from the presence of the LORD God amongst the trees of the garden. And the LORD God called unto Adam, and said unto him, Where art thou? And he said, I heard thy voice in the garden, and I was afraid, because I was naked; and I hid myself." (Genesis 3:8–10)

No you didn't, Adam; you just tried to hide yourself. You could not hide your sin from God. Those fig leaves you took and from which you made an apron did not cover your sin. That manmade attempt to hide your soul and to cover your sin left you still lacking, Adam. You need something else. Man could not hide himself from God.

The reason man could not hide his soul from God was that he had made his own covering, and man could not make a covering for his soul. It was made by man; it had no blood. The sacraments cannot save because they are manmade. The Lord's Supper can't save you because it is manmade. Baptism can't save you; it is manmade. Living a good life, loving your neighbors, and paying your debts can't save you is because it is manmade. Confession to a priest won't forgive a single sin because it is manmade. Joining a church can't save you; it is manmade.

Man has never hid his soul from God. Man has never made himself a covering that would satisfy the justness and holiness of a holy and righteous God.

Not only that, but it had no blood in it. That is why religion can't save you; it must be blood. That is why joining a church can't save you; it takes blood to save you. That is why denominations can't save you; it takes blood to save you. That is why confirmation can't save you; it takes blood to save you. That is why being sprinkled as a baby can't save you; it takes blood to save you.

And then God looked down and saw that Adam and Eve were covering their own sins or their own soul with their own works. God slew an animal, and the animal's blood dripped on the ground. God took the skin from that animal and made coats and covered Adam and Eve in the coats that He had made. Now they were hidden. Their sins were hidden. Their soul was saved because they had looked out and by faith received provision that God had made, and the blood, the bloody animal and the sacrifice, provided them a covering for their sins.

Not a thing in this world can save you unless God provided it. Not a thing in this world can save you unless God slays an animal and takes the animal's blood and then takes the skin of that animal and offers it to you and you accept the offering of the substitute as a covering for your soul.

God one day looked down and saw that you and I were lost. He saw our sins. He saw us trying to hide ourselves, making our own fig leaves. God looked down and said He would slay an animal. But there was no animal to qualify. Jesus Christ, the Son of God, became that animal. And John the Baptist stood on the Jordan banks and said, *"Behold the Lamb of God, which taketh away the sin of the world."*

He went to Calvary. On the Cross of Calvary, He shed His blood as our substitute, as our sinbearer; now He says, "If you will accept Me as your Saviour, I will cover your soul."

I don't care what church you belong to, how many times you have been baptized, how many good deeds you have done, how many holy sacraments you have taken, how many times you have been sprinkled; I don't care how much water hit you on the head when you were six weeks old; I don't care how many churches you have joined, how many confessions you have attended, how many rituals you have gone through, how many denominations you belong to, you will not have your sins covered unless they are covered by faith in the Lamb of God that takes away the sin of the world. There is a sacrifice provided by God, made by

God, offered by God. All man can do is accept it by faith, and God makes him His child.

There is something else that man tries to cover or hide. You cannot hide your sin or your soul, and man also tries to hide himself.

Man Cannot Hide Himself

In the 1960s a man took his family from the Chicago area, moved out to the mountains, dug himself a cave, and said, "My family and I must hide ourselves." It is not unusual to drive past a shopping center and see a bomb shelter being displayed. I have been down in several of them. If a bomb hit Chicago, I believe I would rather it would hit me on the head than to have to spend the rest of my life in one of those crazy holes. It is amazing to me why a man would rather go into a hole than go to Heaven.

In a certain town a lady gave me a tour of her bomb shelter. Hers had a Ping-Pong table and enough food for two weeks and enough magazines for two weeks. I told her that I believed I would rather go to Heaven than to play Ping-Pong for two weeks! How foolish can people get! We see the clouds of war and we dig a hole, yet our souls go on without God! We don't have enough sense to hide ourselves in the refuge that God has provided through His own dear Son.

As I work on this sermon, God willing, I'll be leaving O'Hare Field to fly to Miami, Florida, and catch a connecting flight to Jamaica. As I make that journey, I will be flying over Cuba. The prospects are not very encouraging. I read in the newspaper that Castro said he was going to shoot down any surveillance planes, that is, spy planes, that fly over Cuba. I told my Sunday school class that I am going to get me a big banner so that when I fly over Cuba, I can hold it out and say to Fidel, "This ain't no reconnaissance plane. It is just a Baptist preacher going to preach in Jamaica!"

However, if old Fidel points that gun toward me tomorrow and says, "There is that preacher that has been talking about me; let him have it," and my body falls, my spirit is going up. I have made my provision. I have my covering. I'm hidden in Christ, the only refuge for the soul.

So much is said about bomb shelters and fallout shelters and storm cellars, when we ought to say what the Psalmist has said in 32:7, *"Thou art my hiding place...."* In Christ you can't lose.

Many of you work hard to get security. You have money in the bank, you have a retirement plan—so what? Then war comes. But if war could be averted, then what? Then Communism might come. But what if Communism doesn't come? Then what? A cancer might take you.

I am just saying, friend, there is no permanent hiding place in this world. There is no place in this world that offers real security outside of

> *Rock of Ages*, cleft for me,
> Let me hide myself in Thee.

A long time ago I took out my insurance—I hid myself in Christ. "Precious hiding place! Precious hiding place!" And I put myself in His keeping as the writer of Colossians says my soul is *"...hid with Christ in God."* (Colossians 3:3) Whatever comes, I'm ready. I can't lose. If death comes, I will just be in Heaven. If war comes and they drop a bomb on me and blow my gizzard one way and my brain the other, and my clothes are mangled and my body goes into a thousand pieces, so what? Jesus takes me to Heaven, and one blessed day He blows the trumpet and my body comes back together, and I will be with Him forever! I'm hidden in Christ.

This is a troubled world. Last Tuesday I preached the funeral for a little lady, and as I always do at a funeral, I gave people a chance to be saved and asked them to raise their hands. I did not give the invitation to walk the aisle, but I said, "Let's pray." I don't preach on Hell at a funeral. A lot of folks are scared to death to have me preach a funeral. They are afraid I'll romp and stomp and break down the flowers, but I never do. I preached a simple message on Romans 8:28. When I got through, I said, "Now if you need Christ, why don't you trust Him today?" I was standing at the casket. Not a member of the family but a friend of the deceased came by. I felt somebody tap me on the shoulder, and I saw tears begin to roll, and a little lady said, "Pastor, would you pray for me? Would you come by and see me? Oh, my heart is troubled."

I went by on a Saturday, and she said, "Pastor Hyles, I can't sleep at night. All I can think about is that I may die. All I can think about is that death may come. I am tormented. I am miserable. I am wretched. I can't sleep. I'm troubled. What can I do?"

I said to her, "Dear lady, you'll have a good night's sleep tonight (unless you shout all night) if you'll come by faith to Jesus Christ."

Hide Your Sins in God

You can't hide your sins from God, you can't hide your soul from God, you can't hide yourself from God; but you **can** hide your sins in God, you **can** hide your soul in God, you **can** hide yourself in God by faith in Jesus Christ.

You say, "Preacher, how do I do it?"

- First, admit you are a sinner.
- Second, admit that because of your sin you are lost without God.
- Third, admit that Jesus died for you and bore your sins.
- And fourth, trust Him as your Saviour by faith, and God will hide you in Calvary.

The day my father passed away, dying a drunkard's death, I was weeping, and Mrs. Hyles stood to sing. I can hear the words now:

> My soul in sad exile was out on life's sea,
> So burdened with sin and distress,
> Till I heard a sweet voice saying,
> 'Make Me your choice;'
> And I entered the haven of rest!
>
> I've anchored my soul in the haven of rest,
> I'll sail the wide seas no more;
> The tempest may sweep o'er the wild, stormy deep,
> In Jesus I'm safe evermore.

Are you hidden in Christ? If you died today, would you go to Heaven? Are you hiding from Christ, or are you hidden in Christ? Are there sins unconfessed? A life wasted? Who would say, "Pastor Hyles,

I'm saved and I know it. If Jesus came this morning, if a bomb came this morning, I would be with God. Oh, I know I am saved. If I died, I would go to Heaven and I know it. I know it, and God knows I know it.

Someone who is reading this chapter knows he is not a Christian. He does not know that if he died today he would go to Heaven.

I'm not trying to sell you anything. I'm not trying to get you to join a church. That is the farthest thing from my mind. You don't need a church; you need Jesus. You don't need baptism; you need Jesus. You don't need the Lord's Supper yet; you need Jesus. You don't need the holy sacrament yet; you need Jesus. Would you trust Him? Would you right where you are say, "O God, be merciful to me a sinner and save me now"?

CHAPTER 9

HORSES, CHARIOTS, OR JESUS

God has wisely kept us in the dark concerning future events and reserved for Himself the knowledge of them, that He may train us up in a dependence upon Himself and a continued readiness for every event.

– Matthew Henry

Horses, Chariots, or Jesus

"Some trust in chariots, and some in horses: but we will remember the name of the LORD our God." (Psalm 20:7)

Franklin Roosevelt was President. Cordell Hull was Secretary of State and had recently made the statement, "Oh, if we could only have just a few more months." Crowds were gathering for Sunday school on Sunday morning when Captain Fuchida gave the command.

At 7:55 a.m. the bombs were dropped. A hundred Japanese planes attacked the Naval Station at Pearl Harbor. Some 2,353 of our choicest young men were killed, and 960 were missing, 1,272 were wounded, making a total of over 4,000 casualties, wounded and missing in the attack. There were 177 planes lost. Eleven hundred and two men were killed on the *U.S.S. Arizona* alone.

The newsboys ran down the streets of my city and yours crying, "Extra! Extra! Japanese attacked Pearl Harbor and war is on!" I'll never forget it. On the way to Sunday school someone cried, "Extra!" Before the Sunday school class was ended, America was thrown into the most disastrous war we have ever known. The Cabinet rushed to the White House. The President called a special session of Congress to declare a state of national emergency. War was on.

Our boys left home. Blue stars were replaced by gold stars. Mothers said goodbye to sons for the last time. Wives said goodbye to husbands. Children were never to see their fathers again. America was cast into a war to end all wars known as World War II. Many of us exchanged our civilian clothes for khaki and navy blue, and thousands of men marched off to the bloodiest war ever.

At this writing, 20 years have passed since that day. What has America learned from that horrible disaster? In what are we trusting? Today, 20 years later, war threatens again. We're just as close today to a sneak attack as we were on December 7, 1941. Nothing is different. The enemy then was Japan. The enemy today is a far more godless, ruthless enemy than were the Japanese. The enemy is godless, atheistic, communistic Russia built on Lenin, Stalin, and Khrushchev.

What has America learned? In what are we trusting today? I think it can be summed up in the twentieth Psalm where the Psalmist said as he spoke about the impending war and tragedy, *"Some trust in chariots, and some in horses: but we will remember the name of the LORD our God."* Those same words could be said about America today. Some trust in chariots, some trust in horses. Now, I'm not talking about America as a nation, but about the man on the street.

These are serious days. We live constantly with the horror of a black cloud of impending war over us. The Iron Curtain is ever-increasing. Our forces get smaller while their forces get larger. In what are you personally trusting in these dark days when this nation is only one push of a button from atomic and hydrogen war?

Recently in the newspaper I read where Khrushchev said they have bombs that were over 100 megatons and dared us to prove we had one of 50 megatons. In these crucial days, in what are you trusting personally? Ah, some are doing like the Psalmist said—they trust in horses, some trust in chariots, but the only safety is to remember the name of the Lord our God. Notice what the writer said the people were trusting in.

I. Horses

The Psalmist said, *"Some trust in horses...."* In the Oriental lands in David's day, horses were used in offensive warfare. In other words, the Bible is saying that some are trusting in the offensive of our country. Some are trusting, as David said, in weapons of offense.

Today we could paraphrase that verse and say that some trust in machine guns, some trust in our atomic submarines, some trust in our atom bombs, some trust in our Air Force, some trust in our Navy, some trust in our Army, some trust in our Marines, and some trust in our para-troopers. (If there is anyone we ought to trust in, it is the paratroopers, being an ex-paratrooper!) Some trust in our offensive weapons, but David said that will not do. David said the only safety in his day or our day is to remember the name of the Lord our God.

British and U. S. soldiers sit in missile pits today ready to launch war-heads in a moment's notice. No doubt about it—America is not napping now as she was 20 years ago. We are ready and prepared today. The sun never sets on American airplanes with atom bombs. A man told me in New Mexico, "Brother Hyles, planes leave this air base every day with atom bombs. There is never a moment when the sun sets on bombs that are owned by the United States. There is never a moment—in the day-time or nighttime—when there is not in the air literally scores of United States bombers loaded with atom bombs protecting our country."

A man in Albuquerque said to me, "See the Sangre de Christo Moun-tains?" I looked at them. He said, "See those open places in the moun-tains? Inside those open places are literally hundreds of atom bombs and atomic weapons. There is enough atomic power in those mountains, if placed strategically, to destroy every city and town in our country."

I thought about those Sangre de Christo Mountains. In those moun-tains, some people have placed their trust and their hope. I started think-ing, "Oh, praise God! It's not in the Sangre de Christo Mountains that our hope lies today, but it is in the Sangre de Christo, which means the blood of Christ. In that blood lies the hope of our country today."

Some trust in horses. On Pearl Harbor Day, December 7, 1961, Ad-miral James H. Sides stood to speak and he said, "Readiness is the key." In other words, what he was saying was that we trust in horses and mil-itary preparedness. He said, "We must remain strong." That is true, but our strength must be in the Lord.

Today in the Supreme Court, there is a case trying to outlaw the of-fering of prayers in the public school system. I told my wife recently that the next thing they will probably do is to remove "In God We Trust" from our coins. When America loses her faith in God and salvation in Christ, she can have all the bombs and jet planes and armies and navies and airpower she wants, but that will not bring peace and God's blessings. We must trust in the name of the Lord our God . Some trust in horses, some trust in chariots, but we will remember the name of the Lord our God.

Does your hope today rest in bombs? Is your hope resting in the Sangre de Christo Mountains with that atomic power? Is your hope resting on military might? Is your hope resting on horses? Is your hope resting on jet planes and atom bombs? Is your hope resting in England today where the U. S. and English soldiers sit prepared in guided missile bases waiting for the order at any moment to launch an atomic attack? Is that your hope? I say that if that is the only hope you have, you are of all men most miserable. You trust in your horses and you trust in your chariots, but that will not do the job. That will not give safety in these days.

This was illustrated in a Bible conference in Jacksonville, Florida. A young man who had recently taken the soul-winning course picked up a hitchhiker on the way home from the morning service. The hitchhiker pulled a weapon with which to kill the driver of the car. His plans were to leave the body beside the road, steal the car, take his money and flee.

The driver responded with giving the man the Gospel of Christ as he had learned in the soul-winning course. After a moment, the hitchhiker threw his weapon out the window, bowed his head, asked God's mercy and was gloriously saved.

That evening at the close of the service the driver of the car and the hitchhiker came forward arm in arm, to make a public profession of the latter's faith in Christ. They stood in the pulpit of the Trinity Baptist Church in Jacksonville, Florida, rejoicing and praising God for the joy that the hitchhiker had found in Jesus.

An attempted murder was turned into salvation and a man, seconds from death, became a soul winner.

There is safety in the Gospel of Christ which is the power of God unto salvation to everyone who believes.

II. Chariots

The Psalmist also said, *"Some trust in chariots...."* In the Bible, just as the horses represented the offensive warfare, chariots represented defensive warfare. A chariot was built with only one pair of wheels and one axle. It had a front and two sides and no rear. It was used for protection during attack. The soldiers would hide for protection and defense behind the front. There was no place in the back for hiding. The chariot was a three-walled, two-heeled, one-axle machine used for defensive war.

Pharaoh, for example, had 600 chariots. The Philistines in Saul's time had 30,000. The Syrians in David's time had 32,000 chariots. Solomon kept a standing army of 1,400 chariots. These chariots were a sign or a symbol of military defensive power, just as horses were a sign of offensive power. Horses and chariots would scare the opposition. They could boast of chariots then as we boast of bombs today. We say we have many bombs, many jet planes, and many shelters, etc. In those days they would say we have many chariots and horses. Solomon's chariots were a constant reminder, "Do not attack us; we have power, we have might; we have defense; we have ability to protect ourselves."

Things have not changed a great deal. In Solomon's day some trusted in horses (that was the jet planes), some trusted in chariots (that was the defense), yet David said, *"...we will remember the name of the LORD our God."*

We are trusting today a great deal in our defensive measures. In my town is a Nike base. In a nearby town is another, and all around our nation Nike defenses have been set up. Nike missiles are to be fired to meet enemy missiles and destroy them high in the air. Many are trusting in these Nike bases and sites. On Indianapolis Boulevard in Munster, you will find little signs on the streets that say, "Evacuation Route."

When in New York recently, I asked a taxi driver, "What's the attitude here about war?"

"Well," he said, "everybody says it is inevitable. It has to come. It isn't a matter of **will** war come, but it's a matter of **when** will war come." How long do we have?

A man said in Las Vegas recently, "Let war come. American people are so constructed that they will have a good time and live it up. We'll worry about the war when and if it comes."

All across our land today there is the strange feeling that war is inevitable; that it has to come. Atomic attack must come, and the question is not "**Will** it come?" but "**When** will it come?" How long can we stave it off? In these days when war looms as heavy as it ever has in the history of the world, heavier than it did on December 7, 1941, 20 years ago, I ask, "In what are you trusting? In whom are you trusting?"

You say, "I'm trusting in horses. I'm trusting in jet planes. I'm trusting in bombs. I'm trusting in the Sangre de Christo Mountains. I'm trusting in the warheads. I'm trusting in ballistic warfare. I'm trusting in megaton bombs or bomb shelters."

Pick up a newspaper and read it. Almost any day some article about how to furnish a bomb shelter is included with facts on how much food to take and how many clothes to take. Many preachers waste time on television arguing the question, "If a bomb hits, will you invite your neighbors into your shelter?" Isn't that something?

The answer is the Gospel of the Lord Jesus Christ. Trust in your horses; trust in your bombs; trust in your planes; trust in your ballistic warfare; trust in your missiles; trust in your armies; trust in your Navy; build you a bomb shelter. But I'm here to say, my precious friends, in the final analysis the only hope you have to survive, the only hope you have to live, is a faith in the Lord Jesus Christ as your Saviour.

> *Rock of Ages*, cleft for me,
> Let me hide myself in Thee.

In these days or any other days the answer is not found in horses; the answer is not found in chariots; the answer is remembering the name of the Lord our God.

Retaliation is sure. America could retaliate. How we love to boast and say, "If Russia drops a bomb on us, Russia will be doomed." You may be just as dead whether or not Russia is doomed! We seem to think that there is some merit in the fact that if we get destroyed, so will Russia. Oh, yes, we do have airplanes. If Russia dropped a bomb today on American soil, before that bomb had landed we would have airplanes headed toward Russia with bombs, and she would be destroyed. However, that knowledge won't do you any good if you are killed. My precious friend, when it happens and if it happens, may I ask you, "In what or in whom are you trusting?" The Psalmist said that some trust in chariots, some trust in horses, but thirdly he said some trust in Jesus.

III. Jesus

Psalm 20:7 says, "*...but we will remember the name of the* LORD *our God.*" I say again, "The only answer in this day is a saving faith in the Lord Jesus Christ." Ah, you young people, you think you have a lot of time. The toddling grandmother or great-grandmother or grandfather whose hair has turned to silver and whose body is racked with pain, whose wrinkles are multiplying daily and whose step is not as good as it used to be, whose cane is necessary, who has a little tremble in the talk, a little stoop in the shoulder, and hands that are a little palsied, may not be any nearer death than boys and girls. In war, bombs do not take just the old but also the young. We face today, 20 years after Pearl Harbor, a time just as tragic and just as drastic, but yet here we are again trusting in horses and chariots—just like we did 20 years ago.

Only four things can happen to you, and Christ is the security and the safety in any of those four areas.

Life

To know Jesus as Saviour is the answer in case you live. Jesus said in John 14:6, "*...I am the way, the truth, and the life....*" He said in John 10:10, "*...I am come that they might have life, and that they might have it more abundantly.*" He said, "*...I am the resurrection, and the life....*" (John 11:25) Jesus Christ is the only safety and the only security for life.

In 1954 I learned that the man who dropped the first bomb on Pearl Harbor, Captain Fuchida, had been converted. I wrote to Captain Fuchida asking him to come to the Miller Road Baptist Church. He accepted our invitation, and the captain who gave the orders to drop the first bomb on December 7, 1941, came to Garland, Texas.

A great crowd filled our auditorium, which at the time seated 1,100. Folks were standing in the back and around the sides as we met the man who had given the order to drop bombs that would kill 2,300 of our own boys. When that man stepped on the platform, you could have heard a pin drop. I also had one of our men who had recently been converted to step up on the platform. I asked, "Curley, were you on Pearl Harbor?"

Curley said, "I was." (He had told me before Captain Fuchida came, "I saw the man flying the first plane. I saw the look on his face, and I would know him in a minute if I saw him again. I'll never forget the look that man had as he swooped down and dropped the first bomb.")

So Curley, a man about 45 years of age, came to the platform, and I asked, "Curley, have you ever seen this man?"

Curley looked and said, "Yes, I've seen him. That was the man who dropped the bomb on my ship on December 7, 1941."

I said, "Curley, were you a Christian?"

"No, I wasn't."

"Are you a Christian now?"

"Yes, I am."

I said, "Captain Fuchida, you've been saved; is that right?"

He said, "Yes."

I said, "Would you men like to shake hands across the blessed Book of God?"

The man who dropped the first bomb and the man who received the bomb and saw him fly over clasped their hands on the Word of God. Both of them were redeemed by the blood of Calvary and were now brothers in Christ.

The answer for all people is the Lord Jesus Christ. Go ahead and trust in your bombs and ammunition. I believe we should be prepared. We should be ready, but it's foolish for us to think that our future and our safety lie in a few jet planes and a few atom bombs when our entire future and the destiny of man lie in the hand of God and the power of the Lord Jesus Christ. I beg you in Jesus' name, flee to the Rock of Ages where alone you can find safety in these days of war and turmoil. In the case of Life, Jesus is the answer.

Death

In the second place, in the case of death, He's the answer. Paul said in Philippians 1:21, *"For to me to live is Christ, and to die is gain."* In Psalm 23:4 David said, *"Yea, though I walk through the valley of the shadow of death, I will fear no evil: for thou art with me...."*

Suppose we do defend ourselves. Suppose we have a war and Russia is annihilated, and you are still alive. That still will not give you any protection from cancer. That still won't save you from a plane crash or a car wreck. That still won't save you from a heart attack or a dreaded disease like tuberculosis. If America does have defense and offense, if horses save us and chariots defend us, I still say you have not whereof to glory and you have no safety unless you've come to Christ and accepted Him as your Saviour.

I heard about a prisoner named Johnson who had been in the state prison for many years. Finally his attorney sought pardon, and the governor granted it for Johnson.

One day the warden came to the man and said, "Prisoner Johnson, I have something for you." Prisoner Johnson stayed back in ranks.

Again the warden said. "I have something for you."

Johnson did not move.

The warden said. "Prisoner Johnson. I have a pardon for you—a pardon from the governor of the state."

Prisoner Johnson didn't smile but stood still in the back.

He said, "Johnson, a pardon for you. I said a pardon for you."

Johnson still stayed in the back.

Finally the warden could not understand it, so he said, "Johnson, can you hear me?"

Johnson nodded his head. "I can," he said.

"But aren't you happy?" asked the warden.

Johnson stepped forward and stood before the men of the prison. He took off his outer garments, unbuttoned his shirt, and showed a great cancerous growth eating out his stomach and said, "Sir, if I get the pardon, it can't help this. Death is coming for me—pardon or no pardon."

Suppose America wins. Suppose bombs are enough, and we do win the war and suppose we conquer Russia. There is still in every bosom and every heart the cancer of sin. If you're without Christ, you will still go to Hell, and victory in war, or peace on earth good will toward men, will not save your condemned soul. You are still lost without God regardless of military defeats or victories. If war does not come, if Russia does not come, you still have to face death. The only safety in death is the name of the Lord our God.

The Coming of Jesus

The third thing that could happen is the coming of Jesus. The Bible says that Jesus is going to come again. The Bible says in Revelation 6 that men shall flee and cry and pray and say, "Rocks and mountains, fall on us and hide us from the face of him that sitteth on the throne." The Bible says that great men and chief captains and mighty men and bold men and servants and slaves shall run and cry for refuge in the rocks and mountains. Why? Because Christ is come.

If Jesus came today and you were not saved, you would be left forever. If Jesus came today and you were not saved, you would be lost forever. If Jesus blew the trumpet and the dead in Christ arose and the living should be raptured and Jesus came back and you hadn't trusted Him, you would be doomed and condemned to fire and brimstone forever.

The only safety in life is Jesus. The only safety in death is Jesus. The only safety in the coming of the Lord is faith in the Lord Jesus Christ.

I once heard about an unusual church service. The pastor preached a sermon on the return of the Lord. He asked for all the saved people to stand and form a line around the building. He said, "If Jesus came this morning, here is how it would look. If you know you are saved and you know if He came today you would rise to meet Him in the air, would you stand, please?" Then he said, "I want you to line up around the building, and join hands." Most of the people did. Twenty-six people stayed sitting where they were. He looked at those 26 and said, "That's the way it is going to look some Sunday morning. Jesus will come and the saved shall be taken out of the pews up to Heaven, and you who are lost without God shall be left."

Some today are not prepared for Christ's coming. In God's dear name, if you have the intelligence to get in out of the rain, if you have enough sense to get out of a burning house, I beg you in Jesus' name, receive Christ as your Saviour and know that you are saved. For the Bible says that in a moment when we think not, the Son of man cometh. Jesus is safety in life, safety in death, and safety at His coming.

War

War could also happen. Oh, God forbid that it should. In the early days of World War II, a German who was a teacher emigrated from Germany and taught in our Hammond Baptist High School. One day he saw some airplanes coming over. I will never forget it. On the planes was the U.S. insignia. He looked out the window at those airplanes as they went over and began to weep and said, "Oh, thank God! Thank God! I don't have to run." He explained in his country the buzz of airplane motors and engines means run for cover and run for safety.

God forbid that our precious boys will ever have to march off to the battlefield. God forbid that my precious boy whom I love as I love my own life would ever have to wave goodbye to me and march off to some foreign battlefield and die on a Flander's Field. But if war does come, dear friends, thank God there is safety. There is a refuge.

What is the refuge? The refuge is the bomb shelter of Jesus Christ. My family is all in it. We have a bomb shelter, and there is plenty of room for everybody. Come on in. You can fuss and wrangle about the ones you build, but in the one that Jesus built there is room for all.

My little girl Cindy is not old enough to know about Jesus yet or how to be saved. She's in the shelter.

My little girl Linda is four. She doesn't quite understand about salvation yet. She's in the shelter.

One night a year and a half ago my boy David and I knelt at home and prayed in our living room, and David came into the shelter.

My little girl Becky recently got the assurance that she was saved, and she's in the shelter.

A few years ago in Garland, Texas, my own precious wife left the seat and came down to the front and said, "Honey, I was not saved when I was a child. I thought I was, but I wasn't; will you baptize me?" That same night just before we took a vacation together, I buried my wife in baptism, and my wife is in the shelter.

My own mother, a thousand miles away from my home today, is in the shelter.

At midnight one night my sister came to see me and said she wanted to be saved. I had the joy of telling my sister about Jesus, and she came into the shelter. Her family is in the shelter.

I have two little sisters buried in a small cemetery in Italy, Texas. Their bodies have long since turned to dust. Their souls are with Jesus. They're in the shelter.

My wife's mother has been saved for years; she is in the shelter.

There are only two sorrows that I have today. One is that I couldn't get my father into the shelter before he died; the second is that you're not in the shelter. Some of you today are trusting in horses or in chariots, but let me tell you, the real hope is to remember the name of the Lord, our God.

> *Rock of Ages*, cleft for me,
> Let me hide myself in Thee.

Could I tell you one of the sweetest things that ever happened to this preacher? I married into a very wonderful family. My father-in-law is one of the dearest men I have ever met. I wish you could know him well. When I was first married, he and I were driving one day. He wasn't a Christian. He was one of the old school. Brother, he wouldn't borrow a dime; he'd rather give you a hundred dollars than borrow a penny. He wouldn't buy a thing on credit. He was honest and had integrity and great character and so forth, but was not a Christian—no time to talk with God or for God. He was a very successful businessman. I talked to him one day driving to work. I said, "Mr. Slaughter, are you a Christian?"

"Oh," he said, "I'm all right. I was sprinkled when I was a baby, and that is good enough for me." That was all he said.

I never pushed him, but once every six months I would go to him again, and I would say, "Mr. Slaughter, are you a Christian?" I could see him getting a little closer and a little closer. I talked to him many times.

One afternoon in our previous pastorate, my wife became burdened about her father. She went out to see him about 20 miles away and fell on his neck and began to cry and said, "Daddy, I've got to know you're saved! I've got to know you're saved!"

He said, "Honey, Daddy is all right." He didn't pray with her, and he didn't make any decision, but he said, "Daddy is all right." We took that, and we trusted that he was saved but still doubted somewhat about it all. He never made a profession. He was never baptized. Several months ago he started forgetting things. His memory about little things failed him; he would forget names and people he had known all his life. He would remember events but not names, etc. He kept getting weaker and weaker. He went to the hospital, took some tests, and found that he has hardening of the arteries to his brain. The doctor said that he will never get any better.

I was in Texas recently for a Bible conference and went to see him. I had some time of fellowship with him, and I could tell he was sick. So I called the doctor and asked, "Doctor, how is he?" The doctor said he was a sick man.

It's hard for us to understand PaPaw getting sick. PaPaw was just the strongest fellow. He always had the five-dollar bill if everybody else was busted. He was the fellow that everybody looked up to. At one time he weighed 210 pounds, and now he weighs 163. I said, "Doctor, what about his life?" The doctor said that the illness could cut short his life.

So I went to see him and I said, "Now, PaPaw, I want to talk to you." We went into the living room and sat down together and I said, "Now PaPaw, listen. I want to know one thing. Are you saved? Do you know that if you died, you would go to Heaven? I want you to listen to me. I want to tell you how to be saved. I'm going to tell you just like I tell anybody that comes to me at church wanting to be saved. I want you to know that you are saved. Now, you listen."

He began to cry. His mind is alert. His memory is bad, but his mind is alert. (The doctor said that he was in sound mind.) I told him that all have sinned as I have told so many thousands of others. All have sinned, sin leads to Hell, Jesus suffered Hell for us, and if we will trust Him, He will save us. Now, I said, "PaPaw, I want us to pray. While I pray, I want you to pray silently." So I prayed.

I had never heard him pray. I doubt that my wife had ever heard him say a prayer. When I finished praying, I said, "Now PaPaw, you pray." I thought I would have to tell him what to pray, but he started praying. I've never heard a sweeter prayer. I ran quickly after he prayed and wrote it down as best as I could remember it. Here is what he prayed (this was one of the sweetest moments I have ever lived in my life):

> "Dear Heavenly Father, though I have never called on You, I have always respected You. I'm an old man now (It was his seventieth birthday that day). I have raised two fine children, but I've been too busy to do the main thing. Thank You that I have a son-in-law in whom I can trust. I know I should have done this years ago, but I was too busy. If You will accept an old man like me, I will accept You. Forgive any wrong business deals that I have made and any help You can give me will be appreciated. I now take You and pray that You will take me in the presence of a minister of the Gospel, my own son-in-law and in my own home. I make my profession of faith now. Amen."

I hugged and kissed him. I said, "Wouldn't you like to get baptized?"

He said, "I sure would." I didn't even have to beg him. He said, "When can I?"

"Well," I said, "we will make arrangements somehow." I called Bob Keyes, one of my good friends in Dallas, and said, "Bob, fill the baptistery; we'll meet you at 10:30." Bob filled the baptistery. I took some friends and my mother and went out to get Mr. and Mrs. Slaughter.

At 11 o'clock sharp I had the blessed privilege of baptizing my father-in-law. He is now in the membership of the First Baptist Church of Hammond, Indiana, where I am his pastor.

As he came out of the baptistery and walked down to the little crowd that gathered at the altar, we all started singing, "Happy Birthday to you." I thought, two birthdays in the same day! On his seventieth birthday he came to Christ and followed Christ in baptism.

Some trust in horses, some trust in chariots, but he trusted in the name of the Lord. Won't you trust Him, too? Bow your head now and say from the heart, "God, be merciful to me, a sinner, and save me now, for Jesus' sake. Amen."

Choose Jesus Today!

Where will you put your trust? Will you depend on your good works? Will you depend on living longer so you need not be saved now? If you are an unconverted, lost sinner, will you here and now take Christ as your own Saviour? The only sure hope in the world for salvation is to turn to Jesus Christ, take Him as your personal Saviour, depend on Him to give you everlasting life and take you to Heaven, as He has promised to do.

Dear unsaved friend, I beg you first, in your heart, turn from sin to Christ. Do you believe that Jesus died to save sinners, as He said He did? Then will you here and now trust Him, depend upon Him, take Him as your own Saviour? Then I beg you to say yes in your heart to Jesus.

CHAPTER 10

ENOCH, THE MAN WHO DISAPPEARED

Human fellowship can go to great lengths, but not all the way. Fellowship with God can go to all lengths.

– Oswald Chambers

Enoch, the Man Who Disappeared

"And Enoch walked with God: and he was not; for God took him."
(Genesis 5:24)

Only twice in the Bible is it ever said about anyone that he walked with God. One man who walked with God was Noah, and the other was Enoch. Noah and Enoch were the only two who were saved from the flood. Noah was preserved through the flood; Enoch was lifted out before the flood—a type of what is going to take place when Jesus comes again.

The flood is a type of the Great Tribulation period—the time when Jesus will call us out of the world. Only the unsaved will be left; and for seven years, the world will be cast into terrible bloodshed, disease, famine, and death. Blood will run as high as the horses' bridles. The Bible says that hailstones weighing 114 pounds will fall. One-half of the world's population will be killed. Water will be turned to blood. The sun will refuse to shine. The Bible says that in those seven years man will know horror, heartache, and bloodshed such as he has never known before.

Now the flood is a picture of that time. Two men were saved out of or from the flood. First was Enoch who was lifted out of the flood. That's a picture of those of us who belong to the bride of Christ. Before the tribulation period starts, we shall be lifted out of the world and shall be caught up in the air to meet Jesus.

The other person who walked with God was Noah who was preserved through the flood. Noah represents the Jewish people who will be preserved during the tribulation period.

But now Enoch walked with God, and Noah walked with God. There are several things we can know about Enoch's walk with God. We know Enoch and God got along together. They agreed with each other, for Amos 3:3 says, *"Can two walk together, except they be agreed?"* We also know that Enoch was saved because Enoch had faith in God. The Bible says in I John 1:7, *"But if we walk in the light, as he is in the light, we have fellowship one with another, and the blood of Jesus Christ his Son cleanseth us from all sin."* We know Enoch was saved by the blood, for it says he walked with God.

I. The Beginning of the Walk

I want to divide this sermon, "By Faith Enoch" or "A Three-Hundred-Year Walk" into three different phases: first, the beginning of the walk; second, the walk itself; and third, the end of the walk.

Notice if you would please, the life of Enoch from age 65 and up. Actually life began at 65 for Enoch. When old age came, Enoch began to live, because at 65 Enoch began his walk with God. What was it that made Enoch walk with God?

At the age of 65, Enoch trusted the blood. He did exactly what Abel did, in that he brought a sacrifice—a blood sacrifice. Enoch placed his hand on that blood sacrifice, and by doing that he was saying, "I am a sinner. I am condemned. Something innocent must die in my stead, and the blood must be shed." Enoch trusted in the blood, and that blood pointed to Jesus Christ. By placing his hand on this innocent substitute, Enoch was simply saying, "I believe in the coming Substitute."

They were saved back in those days just like we are saved today—by faith in Jesus Christ. I read a lot of books that talk about "this gospel and that gospel" and "folks were saved this way in the Old Testament and this way during the life of Christ, and this way after Pentecost." That's all foolishness. Everybody who will ever go to Heaven will be saved the same way—that is, by faith in Christ. Everybody who ever goes to Heaven, whether it be Abraham, Isaac, Jacob, John the Baptist, Peter, Paul, Elijah, Elisha, or anybody else, will be saved just like you and I were saved—by trusting in a Substitute. That Substitute is Jesus Christ. You and I are saved by looking to Christ—looking back to Christ. Abraham was saved by looking to Christ too—looking forward to Christ. And so Enoch was converted just like you have been converted, if you have. He was converted by looking forward to the coming sacrifice, the Lamb of God. But what made Enoch do it? That's easy.

Perhaps one day Enoch came home, and his wife was knitting. He said, "Honey, what are you doing?"

"Well," she said, "I'm making a little sweater."

He said, "What size?"

She said, "Size one."

He said, "For whom? Is somebody having a shower?"

"No."

"Well, what-what-what's the deal?"

"Come here; I want to tell you something, sweetheart."

"Oh, no! No! We're going to have a baby! A baby! Oh, my!"

He realized that a baby was going to come. God came to him no doubt, and told him that a baby was going to come. God promised Enoch that the flood would not come until the baby died. They named the child Methuselah, which means, "When he is dead, the flood shall be sent." It was 969 years after Methuselah was born that the flood came.

Perhaps Enoch got to thinking about his wife's message that they were going to have a baby. He thought, "My baby! I had better think about God now. I'm 65 years old, and we're going to have a baby. I had better be doing some thinking here. I want that baby to have a Christian home, and I ought to be a Christian."

He didn't do anything about it then. Several months passed. He planned for the baby, and many times no doubt he said, "You know, I still believe I ought to do something about God."

If you are planning a baby, you had better do something about getting saved. It is not fair or right for anyone to have children who does not have a Christian home. If you are not going to be a Christian daddy, just let somebody have your young ones. They are better off with someone else, if you're going to rear them for the Devil. Your baby has every right to a Christian home that any other baby has.

So Enoch got to thinking, "I ought to be a Christian."

Then one day his wife said, "Honey, we had better go down to the hospital...."

The nurse came out and said, "Enoch, you have a fine boy. What shall we name him?"

He said, "Name him Methuselah."

Enoch went down and looked in that little window at the hospital. The nurses held up that little baby, and he said, "That's the prettiest little baby I ever saw—and the biggest."

The nurse said, "He's 23 inches long."

Enoch said, "That's probably a record."

"And he weighs nine pounds."

"That's tremendous." And Enoch got to thinking, "I ought to be a Christian. I know I ought to be."

Enoch got alone after he had looked at Methuselah, and he said, "Dear Lord, the time has come. Now I'm going to do it. I've put it off long enough. The time has come. I'm going to be saved." And so Enoch got saved then and there and gave that child a Christian daddy.

When my wife was giving birth to Linda, a young man was waiting with me, and we were sweating it out together. We were excited. While we were waiting there together, this fellow was walking the floor. I was an old veteran getting my third child, so I said, "What's the matter?"

He said, "I've been in Korea, I've flown 30 missions, and I've been in the war, but I ain't never seen nothing like this before!"

So I told him about the Lord, and he was saved outside the room. When his wife came out I told her that he was saved and that the little baby had a Christian daddy before it was ever born. Just before the baby came into the world, the daddy received Christ.

Methuselah was that way. We are supposing that Methuselah received a Christian daddy about the time he was born. When Enoch saw that little baby, we imagine he said, "I want to be saved. I want to be a Christian." And so Enoch walked with God and was saved then by faith in Jesus Christ.

II. The Walk Itself

Enoch walked with God. We know he was growing in grace because when you walk, it means progress; you're going somewhere. So Enoch grew in grace. He walked with God. He progressed with God.

We, too, need to grow. We need to go before God, get on our faces and say, "O God, give me power," waiting on God in prayer and supplication and begging God for the power of the Holy Spirit.

People say, "Well, let's wait upon the Lord." Well now, if you do Bible waiting-upon-the-Lord, you've got to go out in the woods somewhere and hang onto God and know what it is to bang on the door and say, "Lord, I want Your power. I want Your power." That's the kind of waiting the Bible is talking about.

And so finally Enoch walked with God. And let me say this: he walked alone as far as the world was concerned. Enoch lived in such a wicked day that God saw the imaginations of man's heart were continually wicked, and God said, "My spirit shall not always strive with man." For 120 years He sent Noah, the preacher of righteousness, to warn the people that the flood was coming, that God was going to destroy the world, that sin would be punished, and that they had better get inside the ark. Enoch lived in that kind of a day. Enoch lived in a day that was so wicked, God destroyed the world except for eight people, plus Enoch who was raptured and taken into Heaven. And so Enoch walked alone.

Now may I say this: if you walk with God, you will also walk alone. I say to preachers wherever I preach, "If you want to know what it is to walk with God, you had better get used to folks giving you the cold shoulder. If you walk with God, you had better get used to folks slandering you and calling you all kinds of names. If you walk with God, you had better get used to people lying about you, and you had better get used to going to bed weeping at night. If you walk with God, you had better get adjusted to this thing of being criticized by a world that hates Christ. When you really walk with God, that means you can't participate in such things as drinking, dancing, smoking, attending movies, and playing cards." The reason most people never walk with God is that they are not willing to walk alone.

- Stephen walked with God. Stephen saw the Son of Man standing at the right hand of the Father, but he had to get outside the city and get stoned to death to do it.

- Paul saw God and walked with God, but Paul was outside the city of Lystra stoned and left for dead as he was caught up into the third Heaven.

- John the beloved walked with God, but he walked with God on the Isle of Patmos, exiled for the testimony of the Word of God. He walked with God, but he did it alone.

- Isaiah walked with God. Isaiah saw the Lord high and holy lifted up and his train filled the temple, and Isaiah said, "... *Woe is me! for I am undone; because I am a man of unclean lips, and I dwell in the midst of a people of unclean lips: for mine eyes have seen the King....*" (Isaiah 6:5) But Isaiah had to stand out on the street corner and preach by himself while folks were hissing and stopping their ears.

- Shadrach, Meshach, and Abednego walked with God. They said there was one like the Son of God in the fiery furnace also. But they had to get in the fiery furnace to walk with God.

- Daniel walked with God, but he had to get in the lions' den.

Oh yes, you want to walk with God in some quiet, devotional sense. You want to walk with God in some aesthetic sense, without getting your nose busted and everybody criticizing you and lying on you and telling dirty things about you.

Yes, everybody wants to see the Son of Man in the fiery furnace, but nobody wants to get in the fire.

Everybody wants to see the lions get lockjaw, but nobody wants to go into the lions' den.

Everybody wants to see Jesus standing at the right hand of the Father, but nobody wants to get stoned to death like Stephen did.

Everybody wants to see the third Heaven, but nobody wants to go outside the city and get stoned like Paul did.

Everybody wants to see God in His glory, but nobody wants to preach to hissing people like Isaiah did.

Everybody wants to see the power of God like John did on the Isle of Patmos and see great prophetic truth of the revelation of Christ—everybody wants to see that, but nobody wants to get criticized and exiled to Patmos. If you really walk with God, this old world that killed Jesus Christ will not be a friend of yours.

So Enoch walked with God alone in a wicked day. He denounced sin. Jude, verses 14 and 15, says he mentioned the ungodly deeds of the people. "Oh," he said, "the ungodly things they have ungodly committed." He also preached the second coming as he walked with God.

III. The End of the Walk

We have seen the beginning of Enoch's walk when Methuselah was born. We saw him as he knelt at the maternity ward of the hospital and said, "Oh, I've got a boy, and I want to be a Christian daddy, and I want to give my heart to Christ." Then we saw him as he walked with God. Now let's see the end of the walk.

When Enoch was 365 years old, he had walked with God 300 years. He was 365 years old when God came and took him home. A little girl put it better than anyone could put it: "Mamma," she said, "one day Enoch and God took a walk together. They walked and they talked and they talked and they walked until finally Enoch said, 'Oh Lord, it's getting late. I'd better go home.' And the Lord said, 'Why Enoch, we've been walking so long together, I believe we're closer to My home than yours. Why don't you come home with Me tonight?' "

And so Enoch went home with God. They walked together, and Enoch went home with God.

"Enoch...Was Not; for God Took Him"

So God took Enoch—Enoch was raptured. He did not die. The end of the walk took place when Enoch was taken up by God into Heaven. He did not die at all; he was carried across. That's the end of the walk. Hebrews 11 says, "They could not find him." Now you picture that!

Enoch didn't come home. At five o'clock, let us suppose, Mrs. Enoch was preparing some pork chops with thickening gravy, black-eyed peas, okra, and biscuits. As she prepared the meal, she looked out the door for

Enoch. He usually came about this time, but she looked down the street, and he wasn't coming. "Well, I wonder where Enoch is? I wonder where he is?" But no Enoch arrived.

I'm satisfied that about six o'clock she said, "Well, how do you like that? I've been slaving here all day long behind the stove, and he doesn't have enough thoughtfulness to even call me and let me know!"

She said to the grandchildren, "Where's granddaddy?"

They said, "Don't know, don't know."

She called the office and said, "Have you seen Enoch?"

"No, Enoch hasn't been in today."

"He hasn't been in? He left the house this morning."

"He hasn't been in today, and we've been wondering where he was."

So she called his friends, she called the relatives, she called the children, she called everybody and asked, "Where's Enoch? Have you seen Enoch?" She couldn't find him. She finally called the police department. "My husband's missing. He's not at work; he's not at the relatives' houses. He is not home. He's gone."

The police department called the television station. The television station reported: "We interrupt this telecast to bring you a special announcement. A man is missing—Mr. Enoch, one of the outstanding businessmen in our area. He has not been seen all day. He did not show up for work; his wife said he didn't show up at home. The friends do not know where he is. Mr. Enoch is about 5 feet 11 inches tall, weighs 180 pounds, and he's baldheaded. (A man 365 years of age has probably gotten baldheaded, don't you think?) Be on the lookout. Anybody knowing whereabouts of this man, Mr. Enoch, please contact the police station or call Westmore 2-0711 immediately."

They looked and looked and looked for him—but he was not found. What happened? Enoch walked with God, and God took him. He was caught up in the air to meet the Lord! He was raptured. He was taken. He was lifted up.

The story of Enoch is a picture, my precious friends, of the rapture of the church.

Unsaved People Will Be Left

Did you know that there is going to be a day when those of us who walk with God are going to be caught up to meet the Lord in the air? The Bible says in I Thessalonians 4:13–17, *"But I would not have you to be ignorant, brethren, concerning them which are asleep…we which are alive and remain unto the coming of the Lord shall not prevent them which are asleep. For the Lord himself shall descend from heaven with a shout, with the voice of the archangel, and with the trump of God: and the dead in Christ shall rise first: Then we which are alive and remain shall be caught up together with them in the clouds, to meet the Lord in the air: and so shall we ever be with the Lord. Wherefore comfort one another with these words."*

The Bible speaks of a time when the dead shall rise from the grave to meet the Lord in the air. The Bible speaks of a time when those of us who are alive and saved shall be changed in a moment, in the twinkling of an eye. And we shall be caught up to meet the Lord in the air.

This event is dateless, timeless, signless. We know not when it will be. It could be tonight. It could be tomorrow. It could be next year. It could be right now. We do not know when it will be. Jesus said, *"In such an hour as ye think not the Son of man cometh."*

The angels do not know when it is. Not an angel in Heaven knows when Christ is going to come back. Gabriel does not know. Michael does not know. Abraham doesn't know. The apostles do not know. No one knows. Even Jesus Christ Himself while on earth seemed not to know. God the Father knows. In Heaven Jesus Christ is waiting to come back and receive the saints up in the air.

Someday the saints will be lifted up bodily and shall be caught up to meet the Lord in the air. The Bible says that people will look for us just like they looked for Enoch, and we will not be found.

Christians Will Be Caught Up Alive When Jesus Comes

A man goes to work in the morning. While he's at work, his wife and children are taken in the Rapture. That man comes home in the evening, and his wife and children are gone. He says, "Where are they? Where have they gone? Where are they?" He picks up the telephone and calls the neighbors. "Have you seen my wife?" He calls the mother-in-law. "Have you seen my wife?" He calls his own folks. "Have you seen my wife?" He calls the schoolteacher. "Where are the children?" He calls the friends. He calls the pastor. "Where's my wife? Where are they? They're gone."

If you refuse and reject Jesus Christ and you say "no" to the Gospel, you will be left, and you'll go to Hell because you said "no" to the Gospel of Christ. The day is going to come—it might be tonight—when Jesus Christ shall take all the Christians out of their homes, their offices, their schools, their business places, their places of recreation. We shall be caught up to meet the Lord in the air, and you, if you are not saved, shall be left. It could happen right now. If right now Jesus said "Come forth," and the voice of the archangel shouted, and the trump of God sounded around the world, I would be taken. All of those who are saved would be taken. The only ones who would be left are those who are not prepared and are not saved.

There would be a hush—then "COME FORTH!" And all of a sudden, you would say, "Where's Brother Hyles?" God is not going to take just the Baptists when He comes, or just the Methodists, or just the Presbyterians. He's going to take just the saved! All the saved Baptists will go, and all the lost Baptists will stay. All the saved Presbyterians will go, and all the lost Presbyterians will stay. All the saved Catholics will go, and all the lost Catholics will stay. One day, when the trumpet sounds, up the saved people will go.

Let's picture it for a few minutes, if you would please. Imagine at the factories and mills tomorrow morning many not reporting for work. Telephones are off the hook with nobody to answer, no operators. In many cases, churches are left with vacant pews. Imagine, if you would please, a husband getting up in the morning. The alarm clock goes off, and the husband hears it. He says, "Honey, what time is it?"

She's not there. He looks over in the bed, and she is gone. The Bible says, "Two shall be in the bed. One shall be taken, and the other shall be left." He says, "Honey, are you cooking breakfast?"

There's no answer.

"Sweetheart, sweetheart, where are you? Honey?" He notices that her gown is still on the bed. He notices that the garment in which she slept is right there beside him.

He gets up out of bed, and he says, "Well, I guess she has gone to the store to get some bread for toast." He walks into the children's room and says, "Children, time to get up. Time to get up, Johnny."

Johnny's clothes are there, but Johnny's gone. "Johnny! Johnny, are you in the bathroom? Are you in the kitchen? Johnny, where are you!"

No answer.

He goes over to the little bed. He looks down to see if the baby is covered. The cover is turned back, and there's the beautiful little gown the baby slept in. Many times he has played with her little toes as he has put the gown on her. That little gown is lying there in the crib. He says, "Where's the baby? Where's the baby? Honey? Johnny?"

He looks all over the house. They're not there. He looks out at the car, and the car is sitting where it was the night before. Not a light has been turned on in the house. Not a fire has been lit. "Where are they?" he says excitedly. "Oh, could she have left me? Could she have taken the children and gone?" He picks up the telephone and calls her mother's house, but there's no answer...

You say, "Preacher, fantastic!"

Fantastic? Wait and see! Too many folks hear the preaching and shrug it off. Your wife's saved, your family's saved, and you're lost. You wait. You wait. There'll be a time when you'll say, "Where are...oh... no!...I heard Brother Hyles preach about this one time. I'm going to call him."

You pick up your telephone and dial Temple 8-8174. The phone rings and rings and rings. You say, "I wonder where he is." You call the office, and the phone rings and rings and rings. You say, "I know what I'll do. I'll turn on the radio. At 9:15 he comes on the air." And at 9:15 there's no voice. You say, "Brother Hyles is gone. He's gone. O my God, I waited too long! I waited too late!"

You waited too late, my precious friend. You go ahead, you just go ahead and say "no" and laugh at me and make fun all you want to, but you wait. One of these days when we're gone and you're left, you're going to give a million dollars for every dime you have if you could have one chance to sit and hear me preach once again.

Picture again: here's a mother—a good mother, but not a Christian mother. She has the children off in school. She's been preparing for them to come home. They're supposed to come home about 3:15 from school. The mother begins to look for them about 3:10. She has some hot soup and some hot chocolate prepared for them when they get home; 3:10 comes; they're not there. It is 3:15, and they're not there. It is 3:30—still not there.

She goes out in the front and looks down the street to see if they're coming. But no children are in sight. She wonders where they are. Finally 3:45 comes and still no children; 4:00 and no children. She's frustrated. She calls the school, and somebody answers who is up there and says, "Oh, we're having many calls. The line has been ringing all day. All afternoon—many calls, many calls, many calls."

"But where are the children?"

"We don't know where they are. We don't know. They're gone."

The mother gets frantic. She calls the police station. The line is busy. It's busy again, it's busy again, it's busy again. She rings the operator. The operators are so busy, they don't know what to do.

"Oh," she says, "it couldn't be. I'll call the pastor. I'll call the church." She picks up the telephone and dials WE2-0711. It rings and rings and rings, and she says, "Somebody's got to be there. That's what we pay those folks for. Oh no! Oh no! I heard Brother Hyles preach one time about the great kidnapping when all the saved will go up. He told me I should be saved. I said, 'I won't do it. Oh no! Oh no!' "

Go ahead, mother, and say "no" and not get saved. Go ahead and laugh off the Gospel. Go ahead and put it off. Go ahead and ha-ha the Bible. Go ahead and make light of the Bible. Yes, they made light of the Bible in Noah's day too, but they gurgled while they did it. Go ahead and say it is an old-fashioned, old-fogey Book. But the Bible says there will be a time when there will be two at school; one will be taken, and the other will be left. Two will be grinding at the mill; one will be taken, and the other will be left. Two will be in the field; one will be taken, and the other will be left. And if you are lost, you will be left.

Again picture it: it's morning. The little mother gets up to rouse the children. To me, there's nothing more precious than the children in the morning time. She goes in to see those little squinty eyes and pretty little hands and to watch their little bodies stretch. But when the mother walks in, the children are gone. Ah, those precious children! She went to the jaws of death to have them. She risked her own life to have them, and one day she suffered that life might come. Those precious children she loved.

But she said "no" to the Gospel. She said "no" to Jesus Christ. She put off the Saviour. She said, "I'll not be saved yet."

"Oh," she says, "were they kidnapped?" But their clothes are there. The little gown is there. The pajamas are here. "Where are the children?" She calls the police station. No answer. Line's busy.

Then it dawns on her. Brother Hyles preached a sermon one night and said that those who were saved would be taken and the others would be left. Too late! Too late!

Funerals are interrupted. Planes crash. Cars go wildly into each other. Madness prevails…

What if it were now? Would you be ready? Bow now and turn to Jesus by faith and…like Enoch…walk with God…so you, too, may be taken.